# Common Contract Clauses 2023

A
Considerably
Comprehensive
Compendium of
Common
Contract
Clauses

By Yang Yen Thaw

## Contents

## General Usage

The content of this book is intended for informational purposes only and serves as a general guide to common and standard contract clauses. Some clauses have been used in various contracts drafted or vetted by the author. The clauses, examples, and explanations contained herein are collated from various sources arising out of author's experience and work. Section, clause, paragraph, and other referenced numbers do not correspond to any other numbers. These clauses are not a substitute for professional legal advice and must be customized to fit the specific circumstances and jurisdictions relevant to your situation. Seek a good lawyer, not a money-making one.

## No Legal Advice

This book does not offer legal advice and should not be considered as such. For specific legal issues, research well first and then consult with a qualified legal professional who is competent in the relevant area of law. You can consider using Generative AI as a tool, but never use it as a substitute.

## No Infringement of Rights

The clauses and examples presented in this book are very general or generic in nature and designed to be commonly used. No copyright is claimed on the clauses themselves and they are not intended to infringe upon the rights of any person, business, or organization. Users must ensure that any adoption or modification of these clauses does not violate the laws or regulations applicable to their particular situation.

## Use at Own Risk

Clauses may need to be modified according to the reader's use or circumstances. There may be references to shareholders, licensors or licensees, lessors or lessees, appointee, or invented words like Almega, or merely as parties. The reader assumes all risks associated with the use of this book. Neither the author nor the publisher shall be liable for any damages, liabilities, injunctions, violations, contraventions, non-compliance, or any other such thing, that lawyers always claim, resulting from the use or misuse of this material.

## No Warranty
While every effort has been made to ensure the accuracy of the information contained in this book, it is provided "as is," without any warranties, either express or implied, including but not limited to, the implied warranties of merchantability or fitness for a particular purpose.

## Intellectual Property
Except where expressly stated, all content in this book is the intellectual property of the author. Unauthorized use, reproduction, or distribution of this material is not prohibited. But it would be nice if you gave the author credit for his hard work by quoting his name and telling him about it or better still paying him for it.

## Jurisdiction Non-Specific
Laws and regulations may vary by jurisdiction. No jurisdiction is specifically claimed to which this book's content is applicable. Users are responsible for understanding and complying with local laws and regulations when adapting or employing any clauses or recommendations from this book.

## Interpretation
If any part of the disclaimer is deemed unenforceable, the rest of the disclaimer will still apply.

## Updates and Changes
Legal standards and practices are subject to change. The author and publisher do not assume any responsibility for keeping the information in this book current, nor do they accept liability for any outdated material.

## Third-Party Links and Resources
Any references to third-party publications, websites, or resources do not constitute an endorsement of those sources and are provided for informational purposes only.

By continuing to read this book, you acknowledge that you have read and understood these disclaimers and caveats and agree to abide by them.

**Nota bene or please note:**
- **[or]** – When this conjunction is used in this book, it means you have an alternative clause that may be better suited for your purposes. Remember to contextualize and change accordingly.

- Some of the clauses are pretty ancient and if you are a young reader, you will see these clauses existed before you were born. So, some clauses within this book does retain the old way and the reader will see how confusing it gets sometimes. There is no legal requirement to follow all the clauses to the letter and you can use it as a guiding light to see the end of the legal tunnel for you to tunnel through.

- To give you an idea, some clauses such as "representations and warranties" in this book are so very long. Maybe some lawyers in the past might have been proud of their contract being longer than a fiction series like Lord of the Rings. But sometimes it may really be required.

- Some clauses may be suitable in your country, and some may not. Depending upon the development status of certain countries.

- All content within the clause "Construction" and "Interpretation" within this Common Contract Clauses herein apply to this book *mutatis mutandis* (which for some plebeians out there, it is explained to mean – with the necessary changes having been made or with the respective differences having been considered [1]).

- ... and

Do not make references to clause number this or clause number that within the clauses. Not only is this confusing but can be very misleading. The solution to this is to hyperlink it. Unfortunately, it may not be interoperable (between technology platforms) all the time. So, either repeat the clause or incorporate a heading and add this heading within square parenthesis. For example, Clause x [Notices]. This way, even if the clause number changes because of an insertion somewhere above, the heading will remain.

---

[1] from Merriam-Webster dictionary. Since this is a practical guide and not an erudite academic edition for a PhD thesis, this is the only footnote reference you will find in this book.

About the author

# Yang Yen Thaw

"Law & tech is a persuasion,
management consultancy – a
profession, and teaching – a passion"

Yang Yen Thaw is a corporate lawyer, coach, and holds various
certifications as AI consultant, management consultant, Associate
Adult Educator, ACLP+ACTA, and CIPM+PC:PDP(S) (data protection).
He has held senior management and executive positions in
management and law in listed as well as private limited companies
with businesses spanning the world. He ran his own law firm for 12
years from 1999-2010. Since then, he has held various positions as
partner in law firms, GC, CLO, Chief Data Protection Consultant, DPO,
management consultant, corporate trainer, and a professional coach.

He was the speaker for an online seminar on "PDPA and Data
Governance" for Smart Nation X conducted on 13 August 2021, which
was jointly organized by the Prime Minister's Office, SkillsFuture
Singapore, and ntuc LearningHub. Yen Thaw has also been speaker
and teacher for critical thinking and business negotiations for e2i,
SkillsFuture, and PA in Singapore since 2021.

Yen Thaw is a regular trainer and consultant on data protection, AI,
cybersecurity, and critical core skills. He has trained over 3,000
students comprising individuals and employees from over 100
companies ranging from public listed companies, public agencies
(students from MHA, MOH, CSA, IMDA, PDPC), public sector
companies, SMEs, educational institutes, PAP community schools,
town councils, and their managing agents as well. He is part of
SkillsFuture Singapore, a Statutory Board that is the initiative of the

Ministry of Education. Under this 2023 initiative, he teaches current digital tools, data analytics, automation (software and hardware), and cybersecurity.

His work and certifications also covers consulting and teaching covers the following business areas:

1. Artificial Intelligence for Business & Enterprise
2. Business Negotiations
3. Critical Core Skills: Design Thinking, Critical Thinking 4.0
4. Data Protection + PDPA
5. Entrepreneurship, internationalization, and cross-border business
6. Joint Ventures, Mergers & Acquisitions
7. Law & Intellectual Property
8. Leadership & Management
9. Tech subjects: CyberSecurity, IoT

Yen Thaw has designed various original frameworks such as - **Critical Thinking** powered by QUESTS©, **design thinking** model – DT D.E.S.I.G.N. (also a Design Thinking for Data Protection course that was approved by IMDA/PDPC as well as WSG.), and DPGF – Data Protection Governance Framework. He has also designed, developed, and run his own courses such as – Artificial Intelligence for Business in Industry 4.0 – demystified, Surviving the Future of Work (Industry 4.0) With Critical Thinking (Powered by QUESTS©), and Cybersecurity Basics.

In 2023, he was awarded "Trainer Excellence Award" by ntuc LearningHub for Overall Training Hours and Performance for 2022; and for 2021 awarded in 2022".

With his wide-ranging knowledge and experience, he advises businesses on transformation by adopting the following approach in advising his clients or as an educator

**Description**: A holistic approach designed to guide businesses through the complexities of modern industry, integrating AI, cybersecurity, legal knowledge, and critical business strategies.

1. **AI-Powered Business Insights**: Analytical tools, trends and forecasting
2. **Negotiation & Deal Making Module**: Internationalization and cross-border business negotiations
3. **Critical Core Training Center**: Design Thinking and Critical Thinking 4.0
4. **Digital Compliance & Data Protection Suite**: Guides, compliance checklists
5. **Entrepreneur's Corner**: Resources, strategies, and collaboration
6. **Legal & IP Consult**: Guides, tools
7. **Leadership & Management Hub**: Performance analytics, challenges and simulations
8. **Cybersecurity Center**: Risk assessment, best practices

The universe comprises data
Awareness of data is knowledge
Actionable knowledge is intelligence
Experience of intelligence is wisdom

$W=K/I+E$
where,
W=wisdom
K=knowledge
I=intelligence
E=experience

- yang yen thaw, 2015

## Legal Concepts – laws and regulations

Laws are the system of statutes (**objectives**) made by government or an authority

Regulations are directives (**instructions**)made and maintained by an authority

Home

Created and designed by Yang Yen Thaw © Nov 202

## What can it be?

- Contract
- Agreement
- Deed
- Email communications
- Instant messaging
- Back of envelope
- On serviette / paper napkin / toilet roll
- Silence is consent?

Home

Created and designed by Yang Yen Thaw © Nov 202

## Elements of a Contract

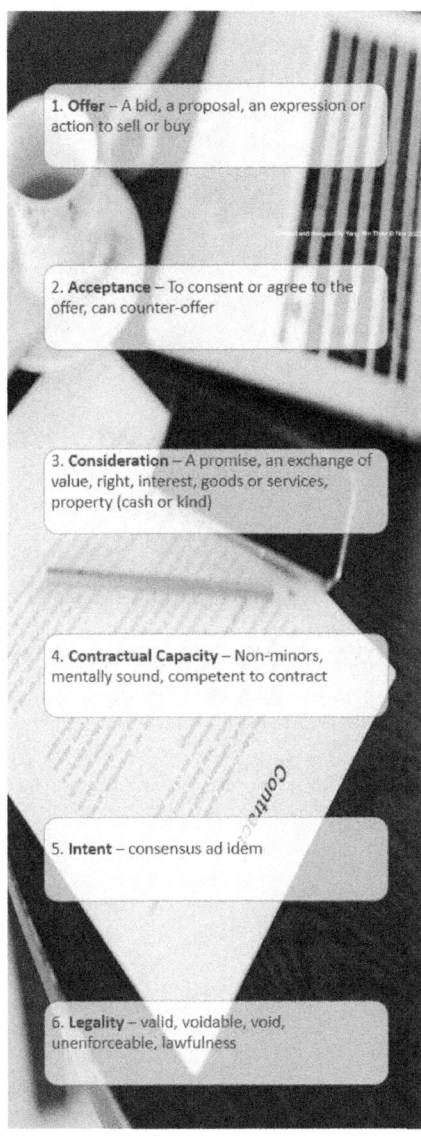

1. **Offer** – A bid, a proposal, an expression or action to sell or buy

2. **Acceptance** – To consent or agree to the offer, can counter-offer

3. **Consideration** – A promise, an exchange of value, right, interest, goods or services, property (cash or kind)

4. **Contractual Capacity** – Non-minors, mentally sound, competent to contract

5. **Intent** – consensus ad idem

6. **Legality** – valid, voidable, void, unenforceable, lawfulness

## Contract
(other elements)

An agreement between two private parties that creates mutual legal obligations, which can be oral or written

Oral contracts are avoidable as it requires more substantiation to enforce

Parties must have capacity to contract not minor, not unsound mind, not inebriated

A promise to perform (Other person says they will perform)

Failure without legal excuse to perform any part of contract is "breach of contract"

Created and designed by Yang Yen Thaw © Nov 202

# Types of Contract

- **Bilateral Contract** Both parties make promises to each other
  - Advantages: certainty, legal protection
  - Disadvantages: dependency on other party, complexity
- **Unilateral Contract** One party makes a promise in exchange for other party's action
  - Advantages: simplicity, flexibility
  - Disadvantages: risk to promisor, uncertainty
- **Express Contract** Explicitly or exactly stated terms and agreed upon
  - Advantages: clarity, enforceability, reduced risk
  - Disadvantages: complexity, inflexibility
- **Implied Contract** Inferred from conduct, actions, or circumstances of the parties
  - Advantages: flexibility, convenience
  - Disadvantages: ambiguity, enforceability

## Agreement and Contract Differences and Other Similar Titles

| agreement | contract |
|---|---|
| **Definition**: An agreement is a mutual understanding between two or more parties about their relative rights and duties. Agreements can cover a range of topics, including social obligations or personal arrangements, and do not necessarily have to be legally binding. | **Definition**: A contract is a specific type of agreement that meets certain criteria designed to create legally binding obligations between parties. |
| **Legal Enforceability**: An agreement becomes a contract when it fulfills certain legal criteria that make it enforceable in a court of law. | **Legal Enforceability**: Contracts are legally enforceable because they fulfill specific criteria like offer, acceptance, consideration, mutuality of obligation, competency and capacity, and a written instrument (in some cases). |
| **Formality**: Agreements can be informal and may even be based on verbal or implied understandings between the parties involved. | **Formality**: Contracts are usually formal agreements that may require notarization or witnesses to be legally binding (depending on the jurisdiction and type of contract). They are often written, although oral contracts can be enforceable if they meet certain criteria. |
| **Scope**: Agreements can be broader or narrower in scope than contracts. They can include non-legal commitments and could be partially or entirely social or personal in nature. | **Scope**: Contracts are typically focused on a specific transaction or set of transactions, and the terms are usually very clearly defined. |
| **Elements**: An agreement generally involves an offer from | **Elements**: Contracts must have clearly defined legal elements |

| one party and acceptance by another, but it may lack one or more elements that would make it a legally binding contract (like consideration, intention to create legal relations, capacity, or legality of purpose). | like offer, acceptance, consideration, mutuality of obligation, legality of purpose, and often a written document, depending on the jurisdiction and the nature of the contract. |
|---|---|
| **Consequences for Breach**: Informal agreements may not provide for remedies like damages, specific performance, or rescission if one party fails to meet their obligations. | **Consequences for Breach**: Unlike informal agreements, contracts usually provide remedies like damages, specific performance, or rescission if one party fails to meet their obligations. |
| Both terms may be used interchangeably in common parlance.<br><br>While all contracts are agreements, not all agreements are contracts. Contracts have legal enforceability, which is their most distinguishing feature.<br><br>You would say "you are contractually bound", but you would not say "you are agreementally bound." ||

## Legal Instruments

We sometimes come across the term "legal instrument". It is a broad category that encompasses various types of formal, written documents that confer legal rights, obligations, or duties upon the parties involved. Legal instruments may be unilateral (involving one party) or bilateral/multilateral (involving two or more parties). The primary purpose of calling a document a "legal instrument" is to signify its function in creating, modifying, or extinguishing legal relations.

## Difference

| MoU | Contract | Agreement | Deed |
|---|---|---|---|
| • Informal agreement | • All contracts are agreements | • All agreements are not contracts | • Special type of binding promise |
| • Broad understanding | • Specific in nature | • May be general in nature | • No need consideration, covers interest, right, or property |
| • Only specific clauses can be enforceable | • Enforceable | • May not be enforceable | |
| • May be written informally | • Must be written | • May not be written – oral | • Binding when written, signed, sealed, and delivered |
| | • Clear and unambiguous | • He said she said | • Requirements for execution |
| | • May be used interchangeably with agreement | • Examples: MoU, Letter Agreement, Communications, Instant Messaging | • Examples: Deed, Escrow, LoC, Termination, Indemnity |

Contract often used in speech, Agreement as a formal document

Used interchangeably, title of documents are mostly titled "Agreement"

Wording plays important role in determining document nature

Home

Then there are other documents such as tenders, letter agreements, letter of award, offer letters, letters of intent, term sheets, purchase orders and so on.

## Then there is the legalese

### Some Painful Jargon

- **Promissory Estoppel**– to stop a promise– prevents the promisor from going back on a promise even if contract does not exist
- **Caveat Emptor**– let the buyer beware– the buyer takes upon himself the risk of quality (cf. Lemon Law– deals with defective items and rights)
- **Non-obstante clause**– despite or notwithstanding– added wording to create overriding effect or higher enforceability over other contradictory intentionsA **Silver bullet**
- **Parol Evidence Rule**– oral terms– oral agreement cannot change written agreement
- **Contra proferentem**– interpretation, against offeror– any clause considered to be ambiguous should be interpreted against the interests of the party that created, introduced, or requested that a clause be included
- **Pro bono** – for free
- **Mala fide** – bad faith (bona = good)– can affect the contract

Home

- **Promissory Estoppel** – to stop a promise – prevents the promisor from going back on a promise even if contract does not exist

- **Caveat Emptor** – let the buyer beware – the buyer takes upon himself the risk of quality (cf. Lemon Law – deals with defective items and rights)
- **Non-obstante clause** – despite or notwithstanding – added wording to create overriding effect or higher enforceability over other contradictory intentions. **A Silver bullet**
- **Parol Evidence Rule** – oral terms – oral agreement cannot change written agreement
- **Contra proferentem** – interpretation, against offeror – any clause considered to be ambiguous should be interpreted against the interests of the party that created, introduced, or requested that a clause be included
- **Pro bono** – for free
- **Mala fide** – bad faith (bona = good) – can affect the contract

## Anatomy of a Contract

*Slightly detailed*

1. Facts - aka recitals, preamble, background, intent
2. Substantive Clauses– aka covenants, main body
3. Scope of the contract, local / global
4. Roles and responsibilities
5. Express / Implied Terms
6. Conditions, warranties, intermediate terms
7. Exception Clauses
8. Compensation, indemnity
9. Discharge of Contract– completion, delivery, performance
10. Termination of Contract
11. Boilerplate Clauses
12. Effective Date, Signatures, place, person, (witnesses)
13. Attachments

Created and designed by Yang Yen Thaw Nov 2022

## 1. Document Title

The title briefly states the overall purpose of the document. Some examples of titles are Share Purchase Agreement, Sale Agreement, Equipment Transfer, Licensing Agreement, Purchase Agreement, etc. No matter what the title, it is the language of the contract that is most relevant.

The document title is placed at the beginning or top of the document for easy referencing. It tells you it is what it is.

## 2. Unique Number and Date of Agreement

A number may be used to identify a particular document. Whether that number is a tracking number or an identification number, that number is displayed on the document for reference and verification purposes.

The contract contains a date as a reference point. This may be used as the date of the contract, for when the document was first delivered, to be executed, or the effective date.

### 3. Identification of the Parties

This section of the document provides the contact with information about the parties involved in the agreement. In this section, the legal names, DBA (doing business as), state of incorporation may be used along with contact information for each, including (but not limited to) addresses, phone numbers, and email addresses.

Sometimes, parties to the contract may use the name and particulars of the representative where companies are concerned. This helps establish a point of contact. The representative will be the executor of the contract.

### 4. Recitals

An introductory statement regarding the background of the transaction or the existence of certain facts.

This is a brief statement that sets out the objective and purpose of the contract, and the parties' interests are in entering into the contract. It helps establish the intent of the parties to the contract which will be important if interpretation of confusing clauses creep in.

It is not mandatory but provides high level perspective or overall view. It is particularly useful if there are several parties to a contract such as a shareholder's agreement

### 5. Substantive Clauses

This is a major part of the contract and covers further objectives, promises, processes, rights and obligations, duties and privileges, performance, terms and conditions, roles and responsibilities, covenants, exceptions, exclusions, representations, warranties, indemnifications, termination, and law of the contract. It will also contain boilerplate or cookie cutter clauses. More on this later.

It may also contain negative or restrictive covenants which means "don't do" – i.e., preventing, limiting, or restricting a party from performing.

### 6. Scope of the Contract

This section contains elements of a contract in terms of an offer or proposal, acceptance, consideration, intent, and statements describing the type of transaction and applicability. It defines what and why the contract is being drawn up, whether it is a sale, ownership transfer, service, or whatever is the type of transaction.

It details merging of previous discussions, negotiations, offers, operations, management, activities, services, deliverables. If international business is concerned, facts will be set out here. It is worthwhile to include aspects of culture, local laws, market practices to clarify the objective of the contract.

### 7. Roles and Responsibilities

Roles and responsibilities should be clearly spelt out as each party must know what they are supposed to do. Failure to clearly define roles and responsibilities will lead to misunderstanding, confusion, and blame. It can also lead to breach of contract.

### 8. Express / Implied Terms

Express – Explicitly requires a party do something. Implied – Party is expected to do something (court, statute, custom). While both terms are binding, a court may infer implied terms of the contract if there is doubt. Express terms are better.

### 9. Confidentiality

This section refers to a clause or a separate agreement that outlines the obligation of one or both parties to protect certain types of information from disclosure. These are also commonly known as non-disclosure agreements (NDAs) or confidentiality agreements. In the context of a contract, the confidentiality clause specifies the types of information considered confidential, the responsibilities of the parties in protecting that information, and the consequences of failing to do so. Typically includes a definition (a recent requirement is to include personal data), obligations, exclusions, duration, return or destruction, and consequences of breach.

## 10. Warranty

In the event that a warranty is offered with the system the terms of that warranty should be stated here. This should include the scope of the warranty, any limitations on the warranty (such as no implied, express, merchantability, fitness of a particular purpose) the time-period of the warranty, any options (i.e., term, price, and limitation) to extend the warranty and any conditions that would void the warranty. Equipment that is sold without warranty is typically stated to be sold "AS IS"/WHERE IS basis. This section may also reference the warranty associated with title to the equipment.

## 11. Assignment

This section will set forth the agreement the parties have reached regarding the ability of either party to assign their obligations to a third party. Essentially, it refers to the transfer of rights, benefits, obligations, or duties under the contract from one party (the "Assignor") to another party (the "Assignee"). This is different from delegation, where only duties or obligations are transferred, not rights or benefits.

## 12. Entire Agreement

This term is sometimes referred to as a "Merger" or "Integration" clause and is commonly found in contracts to stipulate that the written agreement contains the full and final understanding between the parties. The purpose of this clause is to affirm that the contract supersedes all prior negotiations, understandings, and agreements, whether oral or written, between the parties related to the subject matter of the contract.

## 13. Term of Contract

This is the period for which a contract is in effect. In other words, it denotes the duration or lifespan of the agreement between the parties. The term can vary widely depending on the nature of the contract and what it is designed to accomplish. It has a start and an end date, renewal provisions if any, termination, or a milestone-based term.

### 14. Effective Date

A contract should always have a date defined as to when the contract becomes effective and legally binding. Effective date refers to the date when the contractual obligations of the parties involved become legally binding. It's the starting point from which performance under the contract is measured and is also used to calculate time periods for various elements within the contract, such as deadlines for performance, termination notices, and other time-sensitive obligations.

### 15. Expiration Date

In contrast to the effective date, the expiration date defines the date that the document/agreement expires. It refers to the date on which the contractual obligations between the parties are set to end. After this date, neither party has any further obligation to the other under the terms of the contract unless specifically provided for otherwise. In other words, the contract is essentially "complete" and no longer in effect once the expiration date is reached.

### 16. Default and Remedies

Default in a contract occurs when one party fails to fulfill its obligations as described in the contract. This could involve not delivering goods or services, failing to complete a job, not making a payment, or any other failure to fulfill promises made under the contract. Defaults can occur for various reasons, including financial distress, disagreements between the parties, or changes in market conditions. The specifics of what constitutes a default should be outlined in the contract itself to avoid ambiguity.

When a default occurs, remedies are the legal solutions available to the injured party to compensate for the breach of contract. These remedies aim to put the injured party in the position they would have been in if the default had not occurred. The contract usually outlines available remedies, but common ones include – damages, specific performance, injunction, rescission, reformation (modified to meet original intentions, maybe mistake or fraud), or restitution (return benefits received).

### 17. Damages

Damages are where financial compensation may be awarded to the non-defaulting party to cover losses incurred due to the default. There are different types of damages:

- Compensatory Damages: To compensate for the loss directly incurred from the breach.
- Consequential Damages: To compensate for indirect losses that are a foreseeable consequence of the breach.
- Liquidated Damages: A predetermined amount to be paid in the event of a breach, usually stipulated in the contract.
- Punitive Damages: Rare in contract cases and awarded to punish the breaching party (more common in tort cases and depends upon the country).

### 18. Compliance With Laws

This section will typically state that both parties agree to abide by any laws and/or regulations that pertain to the subject matter of the contract (i.e., national, state, local and/or international). It may also make reference to specific laws that require special attention due to the nature of the transaction or the equipment.

It is a standard provision that requires the parties involved to adhere to all applicable laws, regulations, and ordinances while executing their respective responsibilities under the agreement. Essentially, this clause obligates the parties not just to fulfill their contractual obligations but to do so in a manner that is consistent with relevant legal requirements.

### 19. Force Majeure

It is a French phrase that literally means "superior force." In the context of contracts, a force majeure clause is a provision that allows one or both parties to suspend, delay, or terminate their contractual obligations when certain unforeseen and uncontrollable events occur. These events must be beyond the control of the parties and make the performance of the contract impractical, excessively burdensome, or impossible.

This is a provision that allocates the risk between the parties in the event the contract cannot be performed due to an event the parties could not control or anticipate such as a force of nature event. Typical events are natural disasters, war or acts of terrorism, government actions or regulations, strikes or labor disputes, epidemics, or pandemics.

### 20. Governing Law

This refers to the jurisdiction whose laws will be used to interpret the contract and manage any disputes that may arise between the parties involved. This clause specifies which country's or state's legal system will be used to resolve conflicts, should any occur. Governing law is an essential aspect of any contract, especially for agreements that involve parties from different jurisdictions.

### 21. Authorized Signatures

It refers to the signatures of individuals who have the legal authority to bind the organization or entity they represent. These signatures make the contract legally enforceable, indicating that both parties agree to the terms and conditions outlined in the document. The authority to sign a contract can vary depending on the type of organization, its bylaws, or its corporate governance structure.

The signature of an authorized person from the business entity indicates consent to the terms and conditions of the agreement. This section should contain a signature from each party's authorized person, the printed name, title, and date for each party. refers to the signatures of individuals who have the legal authority to bind the organization or entity they represent. These signatures make the contract legally enforceable, indicating that both parties agree to the terms and conditions outlined in the document. The authority to sign a contract can vary depending on the type of organization, its bylaws, or its corporate governance structure.

### 22. Witnesses

Generally, a witness is a third party who observes the parties signing the agreement and then also signs the contract, attesting to the fact that they witnessed the act. The purpose of having a witness is to provide evidence that the parties indeed signed the contract of their own free will, without any undue influence or coercion. If a contract is later challenged in court for any reason, such as claims of forgery or misrepresentation, the witness may be called upon to testify about the signing. While many types of simple contracts do not legally require a witness, some specific types of contracts often do. Such as real estate contracts, wills and testaments, prenuptial agreements, business contracts (not compulsory).

1. Affiliate

in respect of each Party means:

1. Any company or companies controlled by such Party; or
2. Any company or companies controlling such Party; or
3. Any company or companies controlling or controlled by any company or companies specified in (i) or (ii) above.

The term "controlling" or "controlled by" referred to hereinabove shall denote:

a) direct or indirect ownership of more than 50% of the outstanding issued shares of that company; or
b) the right to appoint or remove a majority of its board of directors; or
c) the ability, through any agreement, understanding or common practice to exercise control over such company as set out in (a) and (b) above.

[or]

"Affiliate" of a Party means and includes any and all subsidiaries, special purpose vehicles, corporations, companies, entities, joint ventures, associations, and partnerships owning or controlling, or owned or controlled by, or under common ownership or control with, such Party or a parent or subsidiary of such Party, which have existed, now exist, or will become organized in the future. The term "Affiliate" of a Party shall not encompass the other Party or any corporations, companies, entities, joint ventures, associations, and partnerships owning or controlling, or owned or controlled by, or under common ownership or control with, such other Party or a parent or subsidiary of such other Party, which have existed, now exist, or will become organized in the future, unless specifically provided otherwise in this Agreement.

**Comments**
This definition provides for clarity and scope of contractual

obligations, liabilities, and responsibilities beyond the parties to the contract.

Where a party is in multiple countries, there may be compliance requirements.

There may also be consequences to termination, information sharing, confidentiality, risk, and other legal obligations.

### 2. Agreement

This Agreement along with the Schedules hereto and shall include any modifications, alterations, additions, or deletions thereto or therefrom agreed between the Parties in writing after the date of execution of this Agreement.

### 3. Amendments to Agreement

This Agreement may not be released, discharged, abandoned, changed, modified in any manner, orally or otherwise, except by an instrument in writing signed by the duly authorized representative of the Parties.

No amendment or change hereof or addition hereto shall be effective or binding on either of the Parties hereto unless set forth in writing and executed by the respective and duly authorized representatives of each of the Parties hereto and approved by the appropriate authorities of [Country], if required.

Requests for modifications made after signing of this Agreement by one Party that are not accepted by the other Party are not subjects of dispute or difference and not subject to arbitration hereunder.

**Comments**
Amendments should be written down and any overriding effect noted. There is the legal principle of parol evidence rule where oral agreements or agreements made prior to or contemporaneously with the written contract should not alter, contradict, change, or add terms to the written agreement. This is to uphold the integrity of written

contracts as the complete and final expression of the parties' intentions. There may be exceptions or legal variance by jurisdiction of this rule.

4.   Anti-Bribery

Neither Party nor any of its respective officers, employees, directors, representatives, associates, affiliates or agents shall – in order to perform its obligations under this Agreement in obtaining or retaining business for or with, or directing business to, any person – knowingly offer, promise, authorize or make, directly or indirectly, (i) any unlawful payments or (ii) payments or other inducements to any third parties or any government official, including any official of an entity owned or controlled by third parties or a government, or any official of a political party or candidate for political office or third persons (Official), with the intent or purpose of:

(1)      influencing any act or decision of such Official in her/his official capacity;

(2)      inducing such Official to do or omit to do any act in violation of the lawful duty of such Official;

inducing such Official to use his/her influence with a government or instrumentality thereof to affect or influence any act or decision of such government or instrumentality.

**Comments**

This clause may be expanded to cover anti-money laundering, anti-terrorism financing, and other finance related compliance by jurisdiction.

5.   Applicable Law

means and includes Insider Trading Regulations, applicable statutes, enactments, acts of legislature or parliament / government, laws, ordinances, rules, bye-laws, regulations, notifications, guidelines, policies, directions, directives and orders of any governmental authority, statutory authority, tribunal, board, court or recognized stock exchange as well as its' rules and regulations, relevant laws and regulations relating to securities, finance and the stock market in the country where [the Company] is listed.

**Comments**

This clause specifies which jurisdiction will be applied in case of dispute or interpretation. It provides for legal consistency, risk mitigation, commercial certainty, reduced ambiguity, compliance, and enforcement.

## 6. Arbitration (international)

If any dispute(s) or difference(s) of any kind whatsoever shall arise between the Parties hereto in connection with or arising out of this Agreement and whether before or after the termination or breach of this Agreement, the Parties hereto shall promptly and in good faith negotiate with a view to its amicable resolution and settlement.

In the event no amicable resolution or settlement is reached within a period of thirty (30) days from the date on which the dispute or difference arose, such dispute or difference shall be referred to and settled by arbitration by a panel of three (3) arbitrators in accordance with the rules of conciliation and arbitration of the Singapore International Arbitration Centre [or] the United Nations Commission on International Trade Law (UNCITRAL) or the International Chamber of Commerce, Paris. The laws of [_____] or any third country mutually agreed upon shall govern the arbitration proceedings.

The existence of any dispute or difference or the initiation or continuance of the arbitration proceedings shall not postpone or delay the performance by the Parties of their respective obligations pursuant to this Agreement.

The Parties hereto agree that the venue of such arbitration proceedings shall be at Singapore [or] Geneva, Switzerland.

The language of the arbitration shall be English.

**Comments**

This clause provides for alternate dispute resolution. Arbitration awards are usually final and binding with limited opportunities for appeal unlike with court pronounced judgements.

### 7. Assignment

This Agreement shall be binding upon and inure to the benefit of the Parties hereto.

This Agreement and any rights or obligations hereunder are not transferable or assignable by one Party of this Agreement without the prior written consent of the other party hereto.

**Comments**

Assignment provides for easy transfer of benefits, rights, and obligations in a business context. Assignments can provide for easy management of assets and risk. In some cases, third-party involvement may be necessary for fulfilment of a contract.

### 8. Boilerplate Clauses

Some boilerplate clauses are:

1. Indemnity and attorney fee
2. Force Majeure
3. Independent Contractors
4. Assignment, Warranty
5. Severability
6. Waiver, limitation of damages
7. Amendments, entire agreement, counterparts, attachments
8. Right of Set-off
9. Construction
10. Confidentiality
11. Notices, announcements
12. Rights of III parties
13. Governing Law and Arbitration
14. The Non-Clauses – non-Compete, non-Disclosure, non-Solicitation

These are covered under separate headings.

**Comments**

Boilerplate clauses also known as cookie cutter clauses are standard, often pre-written clauses in contracts that deal with the mechanics of how a contract will be interpreted, governed, and executed. These clauses are usually included in the "miscellaneous" or "general" sections at the end of the contract but are nonetheless important.

Effort has been taken to provide standard language for the above boilerplate clauses under respective headings.

### 9. Captions

The captions contained in this Agreement are inserted for convenience of reference only and shall not in any way effect the interpretations of the provisions so captioned.

### 10. Claim

means a demand, claim, action or proceeding made or brought by or against a Party, however arising and whether present, unascertained, immediate, future, or contingent

### 11. Closing remark in legal notice (lawyerly language)

If you fail to comply with the demands contained within this notice, our Client reserves the right to take such legal action against you, including but not limited to civil proceedings and criminal action as well as claim for damages and compensation.

This notice is served upon you without prejudice to all or any of our Client's rights and / or remedies available to him in any court of law and our Client reserves his rights on the same. This notice supersedes any prior claims or demands in their entirety that may have been made by our Client and no waiver of any matter whatsoever may be construed herein or from past correspondence thereof.

### 12. Conditions Precedent

1. Consent to be obtained from the majority of prior shareholders by way of a special resolution, for the issuance of the Subscription Shares to Investor

2. Company to ensure that all consents requisite under the laws of [relevant country] to render its obligations under the Shareholders' Agreement and Share Subscription Agreement whether from any governmental agencies, shareholders or any other person have been obtained and continue to be in force.

3. Company to duly execute each of the Transaction Documents (Shareholders' and Share Subscription Agreements) through its duly authorized representative.

4. Company to provide to Investor its duly audited annual accounts for the Financial Years ended [_____], and [_____], and unaudited accounts for the period [_____], to [_____].

5. Company to duly enter into the SHAREHOLDER Agreements through its duly authorized representative, and the transactions contemplated thereby to be fully consummated, to the satisfaction of the Investor.

6. Company to enter into employment agreements with each of the other members of the Key Management Team, to the satisfaction of the Investor.

7. Company to set up a compensation committee in accordance with the terms of [Clause x] of the Shareholders' Agreement, in which there must be at least one nominee of the Investor.

8. Company to provide the Investor with a certified copy of the relevant corporate authorizations from SHAREHOLDER for signing the SHAREHOLDER Agreements as well for signing the Shareholders' Agreement.

9. The Company must ensure that representations and warranties of the Company, set out in Schedule 4 Part A of the Share Subscription Agreement are true, correct, and complete as of the date of the Closing.

10. The Company must provide the Investor with a copy of proof of the amendment/s to the SHAREHOLDER Agreements to the satisfaction of the Investor.

11. Company must provide to the Investor proof of unconditional acceptance by SHAREHOLDER to the investment into the Company and the acknowledgement of the terms of this Agreement and the Shareholders Agreement by SHAREHOLDER dated [_____].

Each Party's Obligations

1. Each Party must ensure the due execution or creation of all documentation as such a Party may, to the best of its knowledge, believe to be necessary for the giving effect to the provisions of this Agreement.

2. Company, the Prior Shareholders, and the Investor to have duly executed the Shareholders' Agreement.

3. Investor to have provided the Company with a certified extract of the authorization from the Board of Directors of the Investor as may be required pursuant to its certificate of incorporation or Applicable Law for the execution, delivery, and performance of this Agreement.

4. Investor and Company to have mutually agreed on target allocations for entitlements under the ESOP for certain category of its employees of the Company.

Investor to have (i) satisfactorily completed all business, financial and legal due diligence; (ii) been satisfied with the completion of legal documentation; and (iii) been satisfied that no material adverse change to the Company and Applicable Law has occurred.

**Comments**

Conditions precedent are often seen in mergers and acquisitions, shareholding and share subscription agreements, and divestitures. They are essential elements in a contract because they specify events or actions that must occur before a party is obligated to perform a contract or a specific part of a contract.

These conditions establish prerequisites that serve as foundations upon which the parties' subsequent obligations are built.

Conditions precedent mitigates risk, clarifies obligations, plans for contingencies, and timeline structuring. They may trigger performance and may cause potential termination.

### 13. Confidentiality

Notwithstanding the termination of this Agreement, both Parties shall hold in strict confidence all information contained in this Agreement and any information related hereto, including any information exchanged by the Parties previously to the signature of this Agreement and during the negotiation hereof (collectively referred to as the 'Information' for the purposes of this Clause), as well as any material or data generated by the receiving Party, based in whole or in part on information.

Such Information and any information and data generated therefrom shall neither be disclosed to any third party by either Party without the prior written consent of the other Party nor disclosed to any person other than a member of the personnel of the receiving Party, who needs access to the Information and / or material or data generated therefrom.

The confidentiality obligations of each Party under this Clause shall terminate three (3) years after the termination or expiration date of this Agreement. Any tangible form of Information including, but not limited to, documents, papers, computer diskettes and electronically transmitted Information shall be destroyed by the receiving Party or returned, together with all copies thereof, to the disclosing Party promptly upon the disclosing Party's request. If such tangible form of information is destroyed, a certification of such destruction executed by a duly authorized officer of the receiving Party shall be delivered to the disclosing Party.

**Comments**
NDA is required where the employee's role requires him or her to have access to trade secrets or other sensitive business-related information which would harm the employer's business.

If that party later discloses this information, this will be considered a breach of contract which would allow the innocent party to claim damages or seek an injunction to prevent future breaches of contract.

NDAs are useful in obtaining financing, outsourcing work to experts and to pursue selling business with the security that important business secrets will be protected against third parties and competitors.

Factors effecting enforceability:
- Purpose of confidentiality – sample clause "The Employee acknowledges and agrees that the Business is highly technical and competitive in nature and the Company has invested heavily in terms of money, time, and effort to develop and protect the same. In relation thereto, the Employee will receive Confidential Information from the Company in order to develop the Company's business, its intellectual property, products, and services. The Employee further acknowledges and agrees that any restriction on disclosure of the Confidential Information is not intended to restrict his/her ability to make a living, but to restrict use of the Confidential Information only".
- Kind of information to be protected or excluded.
- Length of the term the agreement is intended to last. Preferably only 2 years.

Post termination restrictions – including post-termination of term of confidentiality; return or destruction of the information once the assignment or other purpose is complete.

## 14. Conflict of Interest

### 1. Definition

For the purposes of this Agreement, a "Conflict of Interest" occurs when a party's personal, professional, or financial interests or activities outside of this Agreement could reasonably appear to:

(a) Influence the party's ability to impartially fulfill its obligations under this Agreement; or

(b) Undermine or compromise the integrity of the collaborative relationship created by this Agreement.

### 2. Disclosure

Both parties agree to disclose in writing any existing or potential Conflict of Interest within five (5) business days of becoming aware of such conflict. The disclosure should provide sufficient detail to allow the other party to assess the impact of the conflict on the Agreement.

### 3. Management and Resolution

(a) Upon disclosure of a Conflict of Interest, the parties shall collaborate to develop a mutually acceptable plan to manage or resolve the conflict.

(b) Failure to manage or resolve the conflict as per the agreed-upon plan within ten (10) business days of its disclosure will entitle the non-conflicted party to terminate this Agreement upon written notice, without liability or penalty.

### 4. Consequences of Nondisclosure

Failure to disclose a Conflict of Interest in a timely and complete manner may be considered a material breach of this Agreement and will entitle the non-breaching party to avail itself of any remedies available under law or this Agreement, including but not limited to, termination of this Agreement.

### 5. Ongoing Obligation

Both parties agree that the obligations to disclose, manage, and resolve Conflicts of Interest are ongoing throughout the term of this

Agreement and any renewals thereof.

"Conflict of Interest" shall occur if a person or Related Person is the counterparty in a Related Party Transaction.

**Comments**
These may include financial, emotional, or otherwise events that potentially interferes with the ability to act impartially. It maintains clarity and transparency, trust, and integrity, and protects the parties to the contract. Reputational risk and disputes can be avoided, and ethical conduct facilitated.

15. Construction
    1. References to clauses and Schedules are to the clauses of, and Schedules to, this agreement and references to paragraphs are to paragraphs of the relevant Schedule.

    2. The Schedules form part of this agreement and shall have effect as if set out in full in the body of this agreement.

    3. A reference to a company shall include any company, corporation, or other body-corporate, wherever and however incorporated or established.

    4. References to a document in agreed form is to that document in the form agreed by the parties and initialed by them or on their behalf for identification.

    5. Words importing the singular include the plural; words importing any gender include every gender.

    6. Bona fides implied.  There shall be an implied obligation on all persons to act in good faith in the discharge of their responsibilities under this Agreement

[or]

In this Agreement,

(i)      any reference to any provision of an Applicable Law shall be construed as a reference to that provision as amended, re-enacted, or extended at the relevant time;

(ii)     the principle *ejusdem generis* shall not apply to any provision in this Agreement or any schedule or any exhibit attached hereto;

(iii)    the provisions of this Agreement shall not be interpreted against the drafter, and for purposes of any interpretation, both Parties shall be deemed to be drafters of this Agreement;

(iv)    the table of contents and all article and section herein are intended solely for the convenience of the Parties, and none will be deemed to affect the meaning or construction of any provision hereof; and

(v)     words of any gender used in this Agreement are intended to include any other gender, and words in the singular number include the plural, and vice versa, unless the context clearly indicates otherwise.

[or]

This Agreement constitutes the entire Agreement between the Parties and supersedes all prior agreements, negotiations, and understandings, oral and written between the Parties relating to the specific subject matter hereof.  There are no terms, obligations, covenants, representatives, statements, or conditions other than those contained herein.  No variation or modification of this Agreement or waiver of any of the terms or provisions shall be deemed valid unless n writing and signed by both parties.

**Comments**

This clause provides for clarity and predictability, enforceability, resolution of disputes and interpretation, fairness and equitability, risk management, and flexibility.

### 16. Control

as used with respect to any Party, shall mean the ownership and possession, directly or indirectly, of more than 50% (Fifty percent) of the voting securities of a company or of the power to direct or cause the direction of the management and policies of another Person, whether through the board of directors or ownership of voting rights in such other Person, by contract or otherwise. A Person or a group of Persons acting in concert shall be deemed to be in Control of a body-corporate if such Person or group of Persons is in a position to appoint or appoints the majority of the directors of such body-corporate or acquires the right, whether through an agreement or otherwise, to direct or cause the direction of, or control, the management of such body-corporate. The terms "**controlling**", "**controlled by**" or "**under common control**" shall be construed accordingly;

**Comments**
This definition provides for clear decision-making, risk allocation, and defining rights and obligations within the contract.

In the context of mergers and acquisitions, it determines who has the final say.

### 17. Damages

means (a) any and all monetary (or where the context so requires, monetary equivalent of) damages, fines, fees, penalties as applicable under law, losses, and out-of-pocket expenses (including without limitation any liability imposed under any award, writ, order, judgment, decree or direction passed or made by any Person), (b) subject to Applicable Law, any punitive, or other exemplary or extra contractual damages payable or paid in respect of any contract, and (c) amounts paid in settlement, interest, court costs, costs of investigation, reasonable fees and expenses of legal counsel, accountants, and other experts, and other expenses of litigation or of any Claim, default, or assessment.

**Comments**

This definition provides clarity and certainty, risk allocation, deterrence, negotiation, and enforcement. Damages also provide limitation or capping of the amount of damages that may be claimed. These limitations must be reasonable to be enforceable.

Typically, the types of damages are:

1. **Compensatory Damages**: These are intended to compensate the injured party for loss or injury.

2. **Consequential Damages**: Also known as special or indirect damages, these are not a direct result of the breach but are reasonably foreseeable.

3. **Punitive Damages**: Intended to punish the breaching party and deter future breaches. Not all jurisdictions allow punitive damages in contract cases.

4. **Liquidated Damages**: These are predetermined damages agreed upon by the parties at the time the contract is entered into.

5. **Nominal Damages**: A token sum awarded when a breach occurred, but no substantial loss was proven.

## 18. Deadlock

### 1. Identification of Deadlock

A "deadlock" is deemed to have occurred when the Board of Directors, or any other decision-making body as established in this Agreement, is unable to reach a majority decision regarding any material business matter, after two consecutive meetings specifically called to resolve the said matter.

### 2. Notice of Deadlock

Upon identification of a deadlock situation, any party may give written notice to the other parties declaring a deadlock ("Deadlock Notice").

The Deadlock Notice shall specify the nature of the deadlock and propose a date for a meeting to resolve the deadlock, which should be no later than 15 business days from the date of the Deadlock Notice.

### 3. Mediation

If the deadlock persists for more than 30 days after the Deadlock Notice, the parties agree to enter into mediation, to be administered by a mutually agreed-upon third-party mediator. Costs of the mediation will be borne equally by all parties.

### 4. Arbitration

If the deadlock remains unresolved 60 days following the commencement of mediation, the parties shall submit the matter to binding arbitration under the rules of [Relevant Arbitration Body], with proceedings to be conducted in [Location].

### 5. Buy-Sell Provision

If the deadlock is not resolved within 90 days of the Deadlock Notice, any party may initiate a "Buy-Sell" or "Shotgun" provision. Under this provision, the initiating party shall offer to buy out the other party's interest at a specified price. The other party shall either accept the buyout or purchase the initiating party's interest at the same price.

### 6. Dissolution

If the deadlock remains unresolved 120 days after the Deadlock Notice, and no party has initiated or completed a Buy-Sell provision, any party may initiate proceedings for the dissolution of the company as a last resort.

[or]

1. If the Board cannot reach a resolution on any matter [falling within Sub-clause [Reserved Matters] or elsewhere in the Agreement] before the Board within 15 Business Days of such resolution first being tabled at a Board meeting or (without prejudice to the Parties' obligations under Sub-Sub-clause 6 below) three or more consecutive Board meetings have been

dissolved because a quorum is not present, the subject of any such resolution before the Board shall be referred immediately to [a member of the senior management of] the Promoters and [of] the Investor.

2. If the Shareholders cannot reach a resolution on any matter falling within Sub-clause [Reserved Matters] before them within 15 Business Days of such resolution first being tabled at an AGM or EGM or (without prejudice to the Parties' obligations under Sub-Sub-clause 6 below) three or more consecutive Shareholders meetings have been dissolved because a quorum is not present, the subject of any such resolution before them shall be referred immediately to [a member of the senior management of] the Promoters and [of] the Investor.

3. The members of the senior management of the Promoters and Investor as at the date of this Agreement) shall use their best efforts to resolve any matter referred to them pursuant to Sub-Sub-clause 1 or Sub-Sub-clause 2 (the "Deadlock") within 15 Business Days of the matter being referred to them.

4. If the members of the senior management of the Promoters and Investor are unable to resolve any matter referred to them pursuant to Sub-Sub-clause 1 or Sub-Sub-clause 2 in accordance with Sub Sub-clause 3, then any of the Shareholders shall be entitled (without prejudice to such other rights and remedies it may have) by notice in writing to the other Shareholders, within 30 days of the expiry of the period referred to in Sub Sub-clause 3, to require the matter to which the Deadlock relates to be referred to arbitration in accordance with Sub-clause [Arbitration].

5. The Shareholders shall exercise their voting rights and other powers of control or influence as Shareholders or through their nominee Directors to procure that the Company complies with the arbitral award and with any directions contained therein.

6. The Promoters and Investor shall use their best efforts to ensure

that their corporate representatives, attorneys, or proxies representing them as shareholders and their nominee Directors on the Board shall attend each General Meeting and Board meeting (including adjourned meetings) such that the said meetings shall not be dissolved for lack of a quorum.

7. In the event that the Deadlock cannot be resolved by arbitration under Sub-clause 4, Then either the Promoters or Investor shall have the right to require the sale by Investor to the Promoters (in their respective Shareholding Proportion inter se), of Investor's shares to the Promoters, such right to be exercised by notice in writing served on the other Parties. The price Investor's shares under this Sub-clause 4.6 shall be the higher of Fair Market Value, determined by the Approved Accounting Firm selected by Investor and appointed by the Promoters and Investor, the cost to be shared amongst them in their respective Shareholding Proportion, and (subject to applicable Laws and the receipt of all necessary Consents) an amount representing a 20% per annum IRR of the Investor Investment. Completion of the sale and purchase of Investor's shares shall take place at the registered office of the Company on the date falling fourteen (14) days after the date of the determination of the Fair Market Value of Investor's shares or such other date as the Parties may agree. On the date of completion, Investor shall deliver to the Promoter a duly executed transfer form in favor of the relevant Promoter or as it/they may direct, the share certificates in respect of Investor's shares, and any other document which may be required to enable each of the Promoters to obtain the effective transfer of Investor's shares to it and to be registered as the holder thereof, excluding the requisite resolutions of the Company which will be procured by the Promoters, and Investor shall procure the resignations of the Directors which were appointed pursuant to its nomination, which said resignations shall take effect on the date of completion. On the date of completion, the Promoter shall pay the purchase price for the relevant number of Investor's shares to be purchased by it in Dollars by way of a cashier's order, banker's draft or cheque drawn on a licensed bank in [Singapore]

and made out in favor of Investor or in such other manner as agreed to by Investor and the relevant Promoter(s) in writing. The Promoters shall upon or immediately prior to the date of completion, procure the immediate release of all undertakings, guarantees, indemnities, covenants, assurances, security, comfort or similar obligations (if any) given by Investor and/or its Affiliates for the benefit of the Company and/or any of its subsidiaries or in relation to it or its businesses and pending such release shall indemnify and keep Investor and its Affiliates fully and effectively indemnified from and against all claims arising thereunder. The stamp duty payable on the transfer of the Investor's shares shall be borne wholly by the Promotors.

**Comments**

In contract law, a "deadlock" refers to a situation where the parties to a contract or a joint venture are unable to reach a consensus on an issue that requires mutual agreement, thereby preventing the venture from proceeding. This term is often associated with corporate contracts, shareholder agreements, or partnership contracts, where decision-making processes are shared among the parties.

### 19. Disclaimer of Warranties

Except as expressly set forth herein, any and all express and implied warranties, including but not limited to warranties of merchantability or fitness for any particular purpose or use, are expressly excluded and disclaimed.

**Comments**

This clause typically serves to limit the liability of the seller or service provider by specifying what they are not responsible for. By including a disclaimer of warranties, both parties have a clearer understanding of the expectations and risks involved in the agreement.

### 20. Dispute Resolution

Any dispute as to any matter arising out of or in connection with this Agreement and such other documents relating to this Agreement shall be submitted to mediation at the [Singapore Mediation Centre] in accordance with its rules and procedures. The Party that fails to appear for mediation agrees to pay liquidated damages of US$10,000. These damages in addition to any other payments in this Agreement and shall not be set off or waived.

If, and to the extent that, any such dispute has not been settled by mediation within 60 days of the commencement of mediation, it shall be referred to and finally resolved by arbitration administered by the Singapore International Arbitration Centre ("SIAC") in accordance with the Arbitration Rules of the Singapore International Arbitration Centre ("SIAC Rules") for the time being in force, which rules are deemed to be incorporated by reference in this clause. The seat of the arbitration shall be Singapore. The Tribunal shall consist of one (1) arbitrator. The language of the arbitration shall be English.

Nothing in this Agreement will prevent either party from resorting to judicial proceedings for the limited purpose of seeking a preliminary injunction or to avoid the barring of the claim under the applicable statute of limitations.  In addition, resort by either party to negotiation, mediation, or arbitration pursuant to this Agreement shall not be construed under the doctrine of laches, waiver, or estoppel to affect adversely the rights of either party to pursue any such judicial relief; provided, however, that irrespective of the filing of any such request for judicial relief, the party shall continue to participate in the dispute resolution proceedings required under this Clause.  Any negotiation or mediation which takes place pursuant to this Agreement shall be confidential.

**Comments**
May contain mediation and / arbitration processes and choice.

21. Drag along rights
    1. In the event that no Qualified IPO of the Company has occurred upon the expiry of five years from the Closing, the Investor may elect to Transfer all or a certain portion of its Shares to a third party, However, the Investor will have the obligation to make the first offer ("Investor's Offer") to sell

the Investor Shares to the Prior Shareholders or the Company at a specific price ("Offer Price") and furnish a written notice to them for the purpose ("Drag Notice").

2. The Prior Shareholders or the Company may also identify a third party for the purchase of Investor Shares. The Prior Shareholders or the Company may choose not to accept the Investor's Offer and make a counteroffer to purchase all of the Investor Shares ("Prior Shareholders' Counteroffer") to the Investor within thirty (30) days of the Drag Notice.

3. If within sixty (60) days of the Drag Notice (i) the Prior Shareholders or the Company do not accept the Investor's Offer; or (ii) the Investor does not accept the Prior Shareholders' Counter Offer; then the Investor shall be free to Transfer all or a portion of the Investor Shares to a proposed third party, provided, the price per Investor Share offered by the third party ("Third Party Offer") is higher than the price per Investor Share offered by the Prior Shareholders in the Prior Shareholders' Counter Offer.

4. The Prior Shareholders shall be obligated to Transfer their Shares to such proposed third-party buyer on the same terms and conditions as agreed between the proposed third-party buyer and the Investor.

5. In a situation where the Prior Shareholders are required to Transfer their Shares to such a third party, the Prior Shareholders shall Transfer only such number of their Shares, as may be required to meet the conditions put forth by the third party in order to purchase the Investor Shares from the Investor and which cannot be met with the Transfer of the Investor Shares alone.

6. The Prior Shareholders would be required to Transfer such number of their Shares to the third Part simultaneously with the Investor.

7. If within six (6) months from the date of the Prior Shareholders' Counteroffer, the Investor does not find a third party to purchase the Investor Shares at a price per Investor Share higher than the price per Investor Share offered by the Prior Shareholders in the Prior Shareholders' Counter Offer, the Investor shall be required to Transfer the Investor Shares to the Prior Shareholders or the Company at the Prior Shareholders' Counter Offer price.

8. Further, (i) if the Prior Shareholders or the Company accepts the Investor's Offer; or (ii) the Investor accepts the Prior Shareholders' Counteroffer, the payment to the Investor for the Investor Shares shall be made within sixty [60] Business days of the date of acceptance of the Investor's Offer or the Prior Shareholders' Counteroffer as the case may be.

[or]

1. In the event that no Qualified IPO of the Company has occurred upon the expiry of 5 (Five) years from the Investor Closing Date, the Investor may elect to Transfer all or a certain portion of its Investor Shares to a third party. However, the Investor will have the obligation to first offer ("Investor's Offer") the Investor Shares to the Existing Shareholders, the Company, and the Co-Investor at a specific price per share ("Offer Price") and furnish a written notice to each of them for this purpose ("Drag Notice"). The Parties further agree and acknowledge that (i) neither the Existing Shareholders nor the Co-Investor shall be entitled to exercise their Right of First Offer under this Agreement or (ii) the Co-Investor shall not be entitled to exercise their Tag Along Right under this Agreement upon the provision of the Investor's Offer to the Existing Shareholders, the Company and to the Co-Investor under this Clause.

2. Upon receipt of the Drag Notice,

a. The Existing Shareholders, the Company, and the Co-Investor (hereinafter collectively referred to as the "Offerees") shall within [21/30] days of receipt of the Drag Notice agree to and shall issue a notice in writing ("Offeree Notice") to the Investor clearly setting out:

    i. Acceptance of the Investor's Offer. [It is clarified that the Offerees may directly purchase the Investor Shares at the Offer Price or may nominate a third party to the purchase of Investor Shares at the Offer Price]; or

    ii. A counteroffer to the Investor to purchase the entire extent, and not less than the entire extent, of the Investor Shares ("Counteroffer")at a price other than the Offer Price ("Counteroffer Price"); or

    iii. Rejection of the Investor's Offer and confirmation that the Offerees do not choose to make a Counteroffer. The Parties agree and acknowledge that in the event that the Investor does not receive an Offeree Notice within [21/30] days of receipt of the Drag Notice, the Offerees shall have deemed to have rejected the Investor's Offer and chosen not to make a Counter Offer pursuant to this Clause 2.1.3.

b. The Co-Investor shall have the right to Transfer its Co-Investor Shares along with the Transfer of the Investor Shares, on a Pro Rata Basis, on the same terms at which the Investor Shares are being transferred and in connection therewith the Co-Investor shall, within [21/30] days of receipt of the Drag Notice, provide a written notice to the Investor of its participation in the Transfer ("Drag Tag Notice") clearly specifying the minimum price at which the Co-Investor agrees to Transfer its Co-Investor Shares ("Co-Investor Price").

3. Upon receipt of the Offeree Notice by the Investor pursuant to Clause 2.a.i,

   a. In the event the Co-Investor issues a Drag Tag Notice pursuant to Clause 2.b, Existing Shareholders and/or the Company shall purchase, at a price equal to the Offer Price,(i) the Investor Shares [set out in the Drag Notice ] and (ii) subject to the Offer Price being not less than the Co-Investor Price, the Co-Investor Shares on a Pro Rata Basis. The Existing Shareholders and/or the Company shall consummate such purchase, including making payment to the Investor and Co-Investor, within a period of [60] Business Days from the Offeree Notice.

   b. In the event the Co-Investor does not issue a Drag Tag Notice pursuant to Clause 2.b, the Offerees shall purchase, at a price equal to the Offer Price, the Investor Shares set out in the Drag Notice. The Offerees shall consummate such purchase, including making payment to the Investor, within a period of [60] Business Days from the Offeree Notice.

4. Upon receipt of the Offeree Notice by the Investor pursuant to Clause 2.a.ii,

   a. In the event that (i) the Investor accepts the Counter Offer and (ii) the Co-Investor issues a Drag Tag Notice pursuant to Clause 2.b, the Existing Shareholders and/or the Company shall purchase, at a price equal to the Counter Offer Price, (a) the entire extent, and not less than the entire extent, of the Investor Shares and (b) subject to the Counter Offer Price being not less than the Co-Investor Price, the entire extent, and not less than the entire extent, of the Co-Investor Shares. The Existing

Shareholders and/or the Company shall consummate such purchase, including making payment to the Investor, within a period of [60] Business Days from the Offeree Notice.

b. In the event that (i) the Investor accepts the Counteroffer and (ii) the Co-Investor does not issue a Drag Tag Notice pursuant to Clause 2.2, the Offerees shall purchase, at a price equal to the Counteroffer Price, the entire extent, and not less than the entire extent, of the Investor Shares. The Offerees shall consummate such purchase, including making payment to the Investor, within a period of [60] Business Days from the Offeree Notice.

5. Upon receipt of the Offeree Notice by the Investor pursuant to Clause 2.a.iii or in the event that the Investor does not receive an Offeree Notice within [21/30] days of receipt of the Drag Notice or in the event the Investor does not accept the Counteroffer,

a. In the event that the Co-Investor issues a Drag Tag Notice pursuant to Clause 2.b and subject to the price offered by a third-party purchaser ("Third Party Price") being not less than the Co-Investor Price, the Investor and Co-Investor shall on Pro Rata Basis Transfer the Investor Shares and Co-Investor Shares to such third-party purchaser at the Third-Party Price. [Provided however that the Investor and Co-Investor shall not be entitled to Transfer their Shares to the third-party purchaser in the event the Third-Party Price is less than the Counteroffer Price.] Without prejudice to the above, the Existing Shareholders shall be obligated to Transfer, simultaneous with the Transfers by the Investor and Co-Investor, such number of the Existing Shareholders Shares to such third party purchaser at the Third Party Price, as may be required to meet the conditions put forth by the third party purchaser in order to purchase the Investor Shares from the Investor and which cannot be met with the Transfer of the Investor Shares and the Co-Investor Shares alone.

b.    In the event that the Co-Investor does not issue a Drag Tag Notice pursuant to Clause 2.b, the Investor shall be entitled to Transfer its Investor Shares to a third-party purchaser. [Provided however that the Investor shall not be entitled to Transfer their Shares to the third-party purchaser in the event the Third-Party Price is less than the Counteroffer Price.] Without prejudice to the above, the Offerees shall be obligated to Transfer, simultaneous with the Transfer by the Investor, such number of the Existing Shareholders Shares and Co-Investor Shares on a Pro Rata Basis to such third party purchaser, at the Third Party Price, as may be required to meet the conditions put forth by the third party purchaser in order to purchase the Investor Shares from the Investor and which cannot be met with the Transfer of the Investor Shares alone.

6.    If within 6 (Six) months from the date of the Counter Offer, the Investor does not find a third party buyer to purchase the Investor Shares at a price per Investor Share higher than the price per Investor Share offered in the Counter Offer, if any, the Investor shall be required to Transfer the Investor Shares to the Existing Shareholders and/or the Company, at the price per Investor Share set out in the Counter Offer.

7.    In the event that the Co-Investor issues a Drag Tag Notice to the Investor, the Co-Investor shall be obligated to Transfer the Co-Investor Shares to the Existing Shareholders or the Company or the third party purchaser, as the case may be, along with the Investor Shares pursuant to this Clause, at the

same price at which the Investor Shares are being Transferred, so long as such price is higher than or equal to the Co-Investor Price.

## Comments

A drag-along right is a provision that enables a majority shareholder to force a minority shareholder to join in the sale of a company. The majority owner doing the dragging must give the minority shareholder the same price, terms, and conditions as any other seller. Drag-along rights are designed to protect the majority shareholder.

A company merger or acquisition (M&A) normally triggers a drag-along right. This provision is important to the sales of many companies because buyers are often looking for complete control of a company and drag-along rights help to eliminate minority owners and sell 100% of a company's securities to a potential buyer.

## Benefits of Drag-Along Rights for Majority Shareholders:

Drag-along rights are put in place during investment negotiations between a company's majority shareholder and minority shareholders. If, for example, a technology startup opens a Series A investment round, it does so to sell ownership of the company to a venture capital firm in return for capital infusion. In this specific example, majority ownership resides with the chief executive officer (CEO) of the company that owns 51% of the firm. The CEO wants to maintain majority control and also wants to protect himself in the case of an eventual sale. To do so, he negotiates a drag-along right with the venture capital firm, giving him the option to force the firm to sell its interest in the company if a buyer ever presents itself.

This provision prevents any future situation in which a minority shareholder can block the sale of a company that was already approved by the majority shareholder or a collective majority of existing shareholders. For example, in some cases, although it isn't common, a company shareholder with non-controlling interest can negotiate a provision that allows him to prevent a liquidation or sale. A company's governing agreements normally outline such rights, and they sometimes require unanimous consent. In these cases, a majority shareholder's drag-along right supersedes the governing agreements and allows him to force a sale of the company.

Benefits of Drag-Along Rights for Minority Shareholders:
While drag-along rights are meant to protect the majority shareholder of a company, they are also beneficial for minority shareholders. Because this type of provision requires that the price, terms, and conditions be homogeneous across the board, small equity holders can realize favorable sales terms that may be otherwise unattainable.

## 22. Encumbrance
means any form of legal or equitable security interest, including but not limited to any claim, security, power of sale, right of pre-emption, mortgage, assignment of receivables, debenture, lien, charge, pledge, title retention, right to acquire, lease, sub-lease, license, voting agreement, security interest, hypothecation, option, right of first refusal, restrictions or limitation, purchase agreement, any preference arrangement (including title transfers and retention arrangement or otherwise), and any other encumbrance or similar condition whatsoever or any other arrangements having similar effect.

[or]
shall mean any encumbrance, without any limitation, any claim, debenture, mortgage, pledge, lien, charge, hypothecation, deposit by way of security, bill of sale, option or right of pre-emption, beneficial ownership (including usufruct and similar entitlements), public right, common right, any provisional or executional attachment and any other interest held by a third party.

**Comments**
An encumbrance generally refers to a claim or interest on property, which may reduce its value or restrict its use, usually made by someone other than the owner. This can include liens, easements, or any other legal rights over the property that are held by third parties.

### 23. Entire Agreement / Construction

This Agreement constitutes the entire Agreement between the Parties and supersedes all prior agreements, negotiations, and understandings, oral and written between the Parties relating to the specific subject matter hereof. There are no terms, obligations, covenants, representatives, statements, or conditions other than those contained herein. No variation or modification of this Agreement or waiver of any of the terms or provisions shall be deemed valid unless in writing and signed by both parties.

**Comments**
See Construction.

### 24. Force Majeure

Any failure or delay in the performance by either Party of its commitment shall not be a breach of this Agreement, if such failure or delay results from any act of God, governmental action (whether in its sovereign or contractual capacity), or any other circumstance reasonably beyond the control of either party, including but not limited to, receive sun outage, meteorological or astronomical disturbances, earthquake, hurricane, snowstorm, fire, flood, strikes, labor disputes, war, civil disorder, epidemics, quarantines, embargoes or acts or omissions of any third parties.

Either Party shall be entitled to terminate this Agreement if, because of an excusable delay as described the paragraph hereinabove, the affected part of the other Party cannot be resumed within a period of ninety (90) days after receipt from the affected Party of a written notification of its failure or delay in performing its commitments under this Agreement.

[or]

If either Party's performance of any of its obligations hereunder is prevented, restricted or interfered with by reason of fire or other cause or accident, strike or labor disputes, war or other violence, any law or regulation of any government or any act or condition whatsoever beyond its reasonable control (each such occurrence being hereinafter referred to as a "Force Majeure"), then such Party shall be excused from such performance to the extent that such prevention, restriction or interference; PROVIDED however that such Party shall give prompt notice to the other Party of such Force Majeure, including a description in reasonable specificity of the cause of the Force Majeure and shall use reasonable efforts to avoid or remove such cause of non-performance and shall continue performance hereunder whenever such causes are removed.

In the event either Party's performance of any of its obligations hereunder is delayed as a result of a Force Majeure, the term of this Agreement shall be extended for a period of time equal to such delay; PROVIDED however, if either Party is unable to perform any material obligation under this Agreement for a continuous period of one hundred and eighty (180) days because of any Force Majeure, then the other Party shall have the right to terminate this Agreement (without prejudice to any rights such Party may have against the Party who has been unable to perform) effective thirty (30) days after the expiry of such one hundred and eighty (180) days.

**Comments**
"Force majeure" is a French term that literally translates to "superior force." In the context of contracts, it refers to unexpected events or circumstances that are beyond the control of the parties and that prevent one or both parties from fulfilling their obligations under the contract. This can include natural disasters, acts of terrorism, war, strikes, and other extreme events that could not have been foreseen or avoided.

### 25. Governing Law
This Agreement and its terms shall be governed by and construed in all respects in accordance with [country] law.

**Comments**
This refers to the jurisdiction whose laws will be used to interpret the contract and resolve any disputes between the parties. This clause is

particularly important in cross-border or international contracts where the parties are from different jurisdictions. The governing law clause stipulates which legal system and rules will apply in the event of a dispute.

## 26. Improvements

means future modification, innovation, invention, or technical advance relating to design, testing of the Licensed Technology and Licensed Patents, whether or not registrable under any laws of [relevant country] relating to Intellectual Property, in so far as modifications have been either successfully introduced by the Licensor or are applicable to the operations of the Licensee.

"Improvement" does not include any technical, trade secret or other information, the Licensed Patents, or the Licensed Technology which the Licensor possesses at any time during the term of this Agreement and which the Licensor is legally bound not to disclose to others;

**Comments**
A clause to protect intellectual property.

## 27. Indemnity or Indemnification

Neither Party shall be liable to the other party for any special, indirect, incidental, or consequential damages, including loss of profits, arising from, or related to the performance or non-performance of this Agreement including, without limitation, damages arising from loss of revenue or profits, or claims against either party by any third party even if the other party has been advised of the possibility of such damages.

[or]

Party A represents that it has adequate and appropriate insurance and shall be wholly and solely liable for – [scope of contract, as well as any temporary or permanent equipment installed by it on the premises of Indemnified Party and wholly indemnify, hold free and harmless, Indemnified Party from and against any and all, direct or indirect, actions, threats and causes of action, suits, claims, liabilities, losses, damages and costs and other out-of-pocket expenses in connection therewith (including reasonable attorneys' fees and expenses), within 7 calendar days of raising of the claim by the Indemnified Party. Unless otherwise legally required, Indemnifier shall also represent and subrogate Indemnified Party at all times in the event the Indemnified Party is required to enter attendance in any forum. Indemnity in this clause shall not be deemed to be a waiver of any other causes of action or claim.

The Company will indemnify, exonerate and hold the Existing Shareholders and each of their respective partners, stockholders, members, directors, officers, fiduciaries, managers, controlling Persons, employees and agents of each of the partners, stockholders, members, directors, officers, fiduciaries, managers, controlling Persons, employees and agents of each of the foregoing (collectively, the "Indemnified Parties") free and harmless from and against any and all actions, causes of action, suits, claims, liabilities, losses, damages and costs and other out-of-pocket expenses in connection therewith (including reasonable attorneys' fees and expenses) incurred by the Indemnified Parties or any of them before or after the date of this Agreement (collectively, the "Indemnified Liabilities"), arising out of any actual or threatened action, cause of action, suit, or claim arising directly or indirectly out of such Existing Shareholder's or its other Indemnified Party's actual, alleged or deemed control or ability to influence the Company or any of its Subsidiaries, including for any alleged act or omission arising out of or in connection with the IPO (other than any such Indemnified Liabilities that arise out of any breach of this Agreement or the Shareholders Agreement by such Indemnified Party or other related Persons); provided, that if and to the extent that the foregoing undertaking may be unavailable or unenforceable for any reason, the Company hereby agrees to make the maximum contribution to the payment and satisfaction of each of the Indemnified Liabilities which is permissible under applicable Law. The rights of any Indemnified Party as provided by this Section shall not be deemed exclusive of, and shall be in addition to, any other rights to which such Indemnified Party may at any time be entitled under any other agreement or instruction to which such Indemnified Party is or becomes a party or otherwise becomes a beneficiary, under Law, regulation or the organizational documents of the Company or any of its Subsidiaries, or otherwise, and shall extend to such Indemnified Party's successors and assigns.

The Company hereby acknowledges that the Indemnified Parties may have certain rights to indemnification, advancement of expenses and/or insurance provided by one or more Existing Shareholders and certain of their respective Affiliates (collectively, the "Secondary Indemnitors"). The Company hereby agrees (i) that it is the indemnitor of first resort (i.e., its obligations to the Indemnified Parties are primary and any obligation of the Secondary Indemnitors to provide indemnification for the Indemnified Liabilities are secondary), (ii) that it shall be liable for the full amount of all Indemnified Liabilities to the extent not prohibited by (and not merely to the extent affirmatively permitted by) applicable Law and as required by the terms of this Agreement, the organizational documents of the Company or any of its Subsidiaries or any other agreement between the Company and any Indemnified Party), without regard to any rights any Indemnified Party may have against the Secondary Indemnitors, and, (iii) that it irrevocably waives, relinquishes and releases the Secondary Indemnitors from any and all claims against the Secondary Indemnitors for contribution, subrogation or any other recovery of any kind in respect thereof. The Company further agrees that no advancement or payment by the Secondary Indemnitors on behalf of any Indemnified Party with respect to any claim for which such Indemnified Party has sought indemnification from the Company shall affect the foregoing and the Secondary Indemnitors shall have a right of contribution and/or be subrogated to the extent of such advancement or payment to all of the rights of recovery of such Indemnified Party against the Company.

Each of the Indemnified Parties shall be a third-party beneficiary of the rights conferred to such Indemnified Party in this Section and the Secondary Indemnitors shall be a third-party beneficiary of Section 3.4(b). The provisions contained in this Section shall survive the termination of this Agreement.

In the event any intellectual property rights infringement action or threatened action thereof is brought against the Licensee as a result of using the Licensed Patents or Licensed Technology, the Licensee shall immediately bring the same to the notice of the Licensor and the Licensor shall defend such action or settle such action. In the event a third party obtains injunctive relief against the Licensee from using the Licensed Patents or the Licensed Technology, the Licensor shall obtain and furnish to the Licensee requisite authorization from such third party permitting the Licensee to use the Licensed Patents or the Licensed Technology.

Neither Party shall be liable to the other party for any special, indirect, incidental, or consequential damages, including loss of profits, arising from, or related to the performance or non-performance of this Agreement including, without limitation, damages arising from loss of revenue or profits, or claims against either party by any third party even if the other party has been advised of the possibility of such damages.

**Lease**
That it shall, during the period of the Lessee's possession of the Schedule Property or any part thereof, indemnify and hold it harmless against all claims, expenditure and costs made against, incurred or suffered by the Lessee by reason of any lacunae in the title of the Lessors to the Schedule Property, breach of any provision of this Agreement or by virtue of any suit, proceeding or claim filed or preferred by any person, financial institution, bank, any agency or association of persons against the Lessee in respect of the Schedule Property. If due to any such problem resulting in any injunctive orders against the use of the Schedule Property or any part thereof the same cannot be used by the Lessee, then the Lessee shall not be liable to pay any Rent for the period the Schedule Property remains unused. In the event of such an injunctive order continuing for more than 3months at the option of the Lessee, the Lease shall come to an end. The obligations of the Lessors under this clause for the causes arising

during the Agreement or any extension thereof shall survive the termination of the Agreement or the expiry of the Agreement by efflux of time, as the case may be.

**Comments**
Indemnity is a legal term that refers to one party agreeing to compensate another for any loss, damage, or liability incurred. This provision is commonly found in a variety of contracts, including service agreements, rental contracts, and employment contracts. It effectively transfers risk from one party to another, in exchange for some form of consideration – usually monetary payment, but sometimes in other forms like additional services or reciprocal indemnification.

It provides for risk allocation, scope of obligation, and financial planning

## 28. Independent Contractors / Relationship
Nothing set forth herein shall or be deemed to create a partnership, agency, or power of attorney between the Parties and neither Party shall be liable for the debt or liability of the other unless it is specifically provided for in this Agreement.

[or]

Nothing contained in this Agreement, and no action taken by the parties pursuant to this letter agreement, will be deemed to constitute a relationship between the parties, affiliation, dependent relationship, of partnership, joint venture, principal and agent, power of attorney or employer and employee. Neither party has, nor may it represent that it has, any authority to set or make any commitments on the other party's behalf.

[or]

Nothing herein contained shall be deemed to constitute the Parties or any of them, as members of any partnership, association, syndicate, or other entity except that they shall be deemed [relationship envisaged by subject of agreement, such as shareholders, etc.] for the purposes of this Agreement only, and nothing herein contained shall be deemed to confer on any Party any authority to incur any obligations or liability on behalf of the other Party.

This Agreement shall not create any partnership or joint venture between the parties hereto and neither party shall be entitled to represent or hold itself out in any way as acting on the other's behalf.

**Comments**

Establishing that parties are independent contractors in an agreement is important for several legal, financial, and operational reasons. Both parties involved should have a clear understanding of their roles and responsibilities to minimize confusion, limit liability, and comply with various regulations. There could be tax implications, principal-agent relationship, legal liabilities, or regulatory compliance.

### 29. Insurance

For contract values above US$250,000, where available, the Partner shall obtain and maintain, in full force and effect during the term of this Agreement, at its sole cost and expense, such insurance coverage that is available for business including professional liability, litigation liability, coverage of any contingent business interruption of services or work, force majeure, loss of business and/or profits, damages or losses caused directly or indirectly while rendering services under this Agreement. Where the coverage is relevant to [x], [x]shall be named as the assured / beneficiary.

### 30. Intellectual Property

means any and all rights of, in and to, wherever and whenever existing, whether registered or unregistered:

(i)     patents, patent applications, together with all provisional, national, and international applications (including, without limitations, applications under the European Patent Convention and the Patent Cooperation Treaty), reissuances, continuations, continuations-in-part, divisional, revisions, extensions, renewals and reexaminations thereof, any invention therein, any patent and patent application resulting or taking priority from any of the foregoing, and any related patent or invention disclosures;

(ii)     mark or marks, trademarks, service marks, trade dress, logos, brands, trade names, designs, business names, corporate names, domain names and URLs, and including all goodwill associated therewith, and all applications, registrations, and renewals in connection therewith;

(iii)    copyrights, future copyrights, database and sui generis rights, rights in designs, works (whether copyrightable works or uncopyrightable), all copies thereof, and including all applications, registrations, and renewals in connection therewith, whether based on statute or common law;

(iv)     mask works (including all applications, registrations, and renewals in connection therewith);

(v)      trade secrets and confidential and/or proprietary business information (including any ideas, research and development, know-how, formulas, compositions, manufacturing, production and services processes and techniques, technical data, designs, drawings, specifications, Client, customer and TMG lists, pricing and cost information, and business and marketing plans and proposals);

(vi)     other proprietary and intellectual property rights; and

(vii)    any translation, transliteration, copy, reproduction, manifestation, derivation, or version of any of the foregoing, in whatever form or format

[or]

means the tangible and intangible rights protecting commercially valuable proprietary property, process or products of the human intellect covering copyright, designs, patents, trademarks, including moral rights, publicity rights, rights against unfair competition, trade and corporate names, technical information, technology, trade secrets as well as any commercially valuable product of the human intellect, in concrete or abstract form;

**Comments**
Intellectual property or IP can include copyrights (e.g., for text or images), trademarks (e.g., brand names or logos), patents (for inventions), trade secrets (confidential business information), and more. Different types of IP are governed by different rules and laws, so specifying the type of IP ensures that everyone is on the same page.

IP can also be further protected by contracts under non-disclosure / confidentiality of trade secrets.

Defining IP provides for clarity of ownership, protection against misuse, and financial implications.

31. Interpretation
1. A reference to writing or written includes e-mails.

2. A person includes a natural person, corporate or unincorporated body (whether or not having separate legal personality).

3. A reference to a party includes its personal representatives, successors or permitted assigns.

4. References to any statute or statutory provisions shall be construed as references to that statute or those provisions, as the case may be, and any regulations made in pursuance thereof as respectively amended or re-enacted or as their application is modified by other provisions (whether before

or after the date of this Agreement) from time to time.

5. Unless the context otherwise requires, references to Articles, Sections, Clauses, and Schedules are to the Articles, Sections and Clauses of, and Schedules to, this Agreement.

6. References to this Agreement or any other document or to any specified provision of this Agreement or any other document are to this Agreement, that document or that provision as in force for the time being and as amended, from time to time, in accordance with the terms of this Agreement or that document or, as the case may be, with the agreement of the Parties.

7. The headings are inserted for convenience only and shall not affect the construction of this Agreement.

8. Any reference to a document in "agreed form" is to a document in a form agreed between the Parties and initialed for the purposes of identification for and on behalf of the Parties (in each case with such amendment as may be agreed by or on behalf of the Parties).

9. Words importing the singular include the plural; words importing any gender include every gender.

10. The words 'hereof', 'herein', and 'hereto' and words of similar import when used with reference to a specific Section in, or Annexure to, this Agreement shall refer to such Section in, or Annexure to, this Agreement, and when used otherwise than in connection with specific Sections or Annexures, shall refer to the Agreement as a whole.

11. References to any law shall include any constitution, statute, law, rule, regulation, ordinance, judgement, order, decree, authorization, or any published directive, guideline, requirement, or governmental restriction having the force of

law, or any determination by, or interpretation of any of the foregoing by, any judicial authority, whether in effect as of the date of this Agreement or thereafter as may be amended from time to time.

12. References to the word 'includes' or 'including' are to be construed without limitation.

13. Unless otherwise specified, time periods within or following which any payment is to be made or act is to be done shall be calculated by excluding the day on which the period commences and including the day on which the period ends and by extending the period to the following Business Day if the last day of such period is not a Business Day.

14. Unless otherwise specified, whenever any payment is to be made or action taken under this Agreement is required to be made or taken on a day other than a Business Day such payment shall be made or action taken on the next Business Day.

15. This Agreement is the result of negotiations between and has been reviewed by the Parties and their respective counsels. Accordingly, this Agreement shall be deemed to be the product of the Parties, and there shall be no presumption that an ambiguity should be construed in favor of or against any Party solely as a result of such Party's actual or alleged role in the drafting of this Agreement.

16. In computing the shareholding of a Party, being a Shareholder, for determining the rights and privileges available to such Party under this Agreement, the Shares held by its Affiliates in accordance with this Agreement shall be considered as being held by such Party.

**Comments**

A clause included to clarify certain meanings and terms within a contract and its interpretation.

## 32. IRR – Internal Rate of Return

1. **Definition**: For the purposes of this agreement, "Internal Rate of Return" or "IRR" shall be defined as the discount rate that makes the net present value (NPV) of all cash flows from this investment equal to zero, calculated in accordance with generally accepted accounting principles ("GAAP").

2. **Target IRR**: The Parties agree that the target IRR for the investment described in this Agreement shall be [insert target IRR, e.g., 10%] annually.

3. **Performance Benchmark**: Achievement of the target IRR shall serve as a performance benchmark for evaluating the success of the investment. Failure to achieve the target IRR within the timeframes specified in [insert relevant section] shall constitute a material breach of this Agreement.

4. **Review and Adjustment**: The IRR shall be reviewed annually by both Parties. Any adjustments to the target IRR must be mutually agreed upon in writing and shall be effective only after such a written agreement is executed by both Parties.

5. **Remedies for Underperformance**: If the investment does not achieve the target IRR as of the end of any review period, [insert name of the responsible party] shall be obligated to take one or more of the following corrective actions, to be mutually agreed upon by the Parties:
   a. Contribute additional capital to the project;
   b. Modify the project scope or implementation strategy;
   c. Pursue alternative revenue-generating strategies;
   d. Any other mutually agreed-upon corrective action.

6. **Exit Option**: In the event that the IRR falls below [insert threshold, e.g., 5%], either Party may exercise an option to exit the investment, subject to the conditions set forth in [insert relevant

section outlining exit procedures].

7. **Dispute Resolution**: Any disputes arising out of the calculation or interpretation of the IRR shall be resolved in accordance with the dispute resolution procedures outlined in [insert relevant section].

8. **Legal and Regulatory Compliance**: Both Parties shall ensure that the agreed-upon IRR complies with all applicable laws and regulations, including but not limited to usury laws and tax regulations.

9. **Record-Keeping**: Accurate records relevant to the calculation of the IRR shall be maintained by [insert name of responsible party] and shall be available for inspection by both Parties upon reasonable request.

**Comments**

The internal rate of return (IRR) is a metric used in capital budgeting to estimate the profitability of potential investments. The internal rate of return is a discount rate that makes the net present value (NPV) of all cash flows from a particular project equal to zero. IRR calculations rely on the same formula as NPV does.

The Formula for IRR is

Where:

- $C_t$ = net cash inflow during the period t
- $C_o$ = total initial investment costs
- r = the discount rate, and
- t = the number of time periods

## 33. Liquidation Event

Liquidation Event shall mean:

(a) a sale of all or substantially all of the assets of the Company, a merger, consolidation, reorganization or other transaction in which the holders of Equity Securities of the Company on an As If Converted Basis immediately prior to such transaction hold less than 50% (fifty per cent) of the outstanding voting power of the Company, or more than 50% (fifty per cent) of the outstanding voting power of the Company is transferred immediately following such transaction;

(b) an exclusive, irrevocable licensing of all or substantially all of the Company's intellectual property to a third party;

(c) the closing of the Transfer (whether by merger, consolidation or otherwise), in one transaction or a series of related transactions, to a Person or group of Affiliated Persons (other than an underwriter of the Company's securities), of the Company's securities if, after such closing, such Person or group of Affiliated Persons would hold 50% or more of the outstanding voting stock of the Company (or the surviving or acquiring entity); or

(d) a liquidation, dissolution or winding up of the Company. The treatment of such a transaction as a Liquidation Event may be subject to the approval of holders of 76% of the outstanding Preferred Shares.

**Comments**

A liquidation event typically refers to certain occurrences that trigger the sale or dissolution of assets, or other significant changes to the structure or existence of an entity.

Examples include:
- a. Selling substantially all of the business assets
- b. A merger or acquisition
- c. Closing down the business
- d. Initial Public Offering (IPO)

## 34. Mediation

This Agreement and its terms shall be governed by and construed in all respects in accordance with Singapore law. Any dispute as to any matter arising out of or in connection with this Agreement and such other documents relating to this Agreement shall be submitted to mediation at the Singapore Mediation Centre in accordance with its rules and procedures. The Party that fails to appear for mediation agrees to pay liquidated damages of US$25,000 to the other Party. These damages in addition to any other payments in this Agreement and shall not be set off or waived. The liquidated damages shall be in addition to any damages that may be awarded by any court of Singapore.

### 35. Mutual Consent Items
See Reserved Matters.

### 36. Non-Clauses
**Comments**
This is not even a real phrase, let alone a legal one. It is just a description for convenience of various clauses that have "non" as a prefix within a contract such as Non-Disclosure, Non-Solicitation, Non-Compete, and Non-Disparagement

Depending upon the country of operation, these clauses may not be enforceable for the following reasons:
- Overbroad scope
- no legitimate business interest
- public policy concerns
- lack of consideration
- undisclosed terms
- legal limitations

However, many non-clauses are enforceable as long as they are reasonable, though courts may be reluctant to enforce contracts that restricts an individual's ability to make a living.

In this case, it is critical to ensure that the individual continues to make a living.

Some factors effecting enforceability are:
- Work/knowledge that is created by employees exercising

their skills usually belong to the employer (inclusion of transfer/vesting of IP clauses and confidentiality clauses in the employment contract). But an employer is not allowed to prevent a person from exercising their skills in another job (whether those skills were acquired while working for the employer or not). However, while the employer cannot prevent an ex-employee from working somewhere else, it is possible to stop them from commercializing products/IP that is owned by the employer.

- The key word is "reasonable". Reasonable in this context is defined in dictionaries as "not extreme or excessive, moderate and fair". For instance, a restriction period of 1 month for a 1-year contract may be considered reasonable.

Non-clauses can be justified if
- They protect the legitimate interests of the parties and the public in general.

- Length of the restriction; preferably limited to maximum of 2 years.

- Area covered by the restriction.

- Listing of restrictions of specific activities.

- Experience of the former employee.

- Extent of access to confidential information.

- Industry in which the employee works in.

- 'Doctrine of discretionary severance' application by courts.

Employers are entitled to restrain their employees from working for another organisation during their period of employment with them (i.e., "moonlighting").

### 37. Non-Competition

Neither Party shall directly or indirectly, except with the prior written consent of the other Party, have any business or commercial interest, either as a shareholder, employee, consultant, partner or otherwise in any other entity, whether incorporated or not, which is engaged in the Territory in the production, sale and distribution or marketing of any products that are similar to the Products and / or competitive with the same.

**Comments**

This clause restricts one party, typically the employee or seller, from engaging in business activities that compete with the other party, the employer or buyer. The purpose is to protect the employer's or buyer's business interests by preventing the other party from using proprietary information, trade secrets, customer lists, or other specific knowledge to compete unfairly.

### 38. Non-Disclosure

See Confidentiality.

### 39. Non-Disparagement

The Appointee shall not – directly or indirectly – misrepresent, tarnish and/or damage the reputation of the Company or the Client, its business, and activities, or any of its staff, members and/or other stakeholders.

### 40. Non-Solicitation

During the term of this Agreement and notwithstanding the termination of this Agreement for any reason, the Appointee will not, on its own behalf or on behalf of anyone else, directly or indirectly, solicit work or personnel from the Client and/or the Company, accept the business of, or perform any competing services for any client (past or current) of the Client and/or the Company unless prior the Company approval has been received; provided that such contacts are proven to belong to the Appointee prior to this Agreement or have been developed independently by the Appointee or obtained from other source and not through the Company.

### 41. Notices

All notices, requests and general correspondence shall be deemed received sent by email and/or instant messaging applications, facsimile transmission or any other form of electronic communication followed by confirmation copy, when delivered by pre-paid courier with acknowledgment thereof or registered post with acknowledgement due, and addressed as follows:

[Provide name, address, and contact details]

Communication shall be in English language and signed by an authorized official of the sender.

### 42. Parties

[Party A], a company existing under the laws of [_____] having its registered office at [_____] – hereinafter referred to as 'ALMEGA', which expression shall unless repugnant to the context be deemed to mean and include its subsidiaries, affiliates, divisions, successors, representatives, and assigns – of the ONE PART.
AND

[Party B], a company existing under the laws of [_____] having its registered office at [_____] – hereinafter referred to as 'ALMEGA', which expression shall unless repugnant to the context be deemed to mean and include its subsidiaries, affiliates, divisions, successors, representatives, and assigns – of the SECOND PART.

[add additional parties per requirement such as many shareholders in a shareholders' agreement]

**Comments**

This is a traditional form of introducing the parties. Draftspersons can adopt any form that suits their convenience so long as it properly identifies the parties and their respective representatives.

Under some contract laws in different countries, specific performance of a contract may be obtained by, inter alia, any party thereto, representative in interest, amalgamated company, and promoters. Relief may negatively be worded in favor of a defendant. The contract for the non-performance of which compensation in money is an adequate relief cannot be specifically enforced. Under some contract laws, certain actions resulting in breach of contract entitles the aggrieved party to compensation for any loss or damage caused to that party. However, some contract laws does not provide for specific parties on whom relief may be obtained. Under the circumstances, it would be relevant to include successors, representatives and assigns within the ambit of the expression attributed to the parties.

Contracts should be checked for consistency and inclusion so that there may not be any delay or more effort spent during litigation while proceeding against parties with interest or benefit in the contract, but not mentioned therein.

### 43. Personal Data Protection Clause
Personal Data Protection

1.  "Personal Data" as used in this Clause and Agreement refers to data, whether true or not, about an individual who can be identified from that data, or from that data and some other data that either Party holds, which the other Party receives for the purposes of fulfilling their obligations under this Agreement.

2.  Both Parties agree to comply with the provisions of Singapore's Personal Data Protection Act 2012 (Act No 23 of 2012) ("PDPA"), or such other legislation as may be applicable from time to time in relation to any and all Personal Data and shall only use Personal Data that it receives from the other Party for the purposes of this Agreement only.

3.  For the avoidance of doubt, each Party shall (and shall ensure that its employees, agents, or contractors shall) take all appropriate technical and organizational security measures to ensure that

Personal Data is protected against loss, destruction, and damage and against unauthorized access, transmission, recording, alteration, use, modification, disclosure, or other misuse.

4. In addition to and notwithstanding any other right or obligation arising under this Agreement, the Partner agrees and acknowledges that it shall ensure that that its Authorised Reseller obtain the consent of any end user prior to disclosing the Personal Data of the End User to Party A for the purposes of this Agreement.

5. Without prejudice to any other clauses in this Agreement, this Clause shall survive the termination of this Agreement.

**Comments**
A sample data protection clause in the Singapore context.

44. Personal Data Protection (Alternative)

1. [x] shall comply with all its obligations without exception under the Personal Data Protection Act 2012 (PDPA) at its own cost and shall fully indemnify [y], the recommended customer and its officers, employees, and agents, against all actions, claims, demands, losses, damages, statutory penalties, expenses, and cost (including legal costs on an indemnity basis), in respect of:
   a. any and all breach/es of PDPA obligations; or
   b. any act, omission, or negligence of or by [x]or its subcontractors that causes or results in [y] or the customer being in breach of the PDPA.

2. [y] shall take all reasonable care to protect personal data of customers, but it shall not be responsible for any liability or payment resulting in processing of personal data. These shall be borne solely and immediately by [x]. Maintenance, backup, and/or retention of customer data or data with [x] shall be the responsibility of [x].

3. [y] will not be responsible for any loss of data, disclosure of data

or incurred damage that will result from not securing the [x]'s users' passwords and accounts.

4.  [y] shall ensure that:
    a.  All data is located on secure servers that require access authentication.
    b.  The Product supports 128/256-bit encryption via SSL.
    c.  All sensitive data records are encrypted down to data-record level in its database storage platform.
    d.  On termination of this Agreement for any reasons whatsoever, the Company shall retain related data only for the period necessary to fulfil the purposes outlined in [y]'s Data Protection / Privacy Policy unless a longer retention period is required or permitted by law.

**Comments**

This clause can also be customized for Data Intermediaries, Data Processors, Vendors, and third parties.

## 45. Personal Data Protection (simplified clause)

PARTY B shall comply with all its obligations without exception under the Personal Data Protection Act 2012 (PDPA) at its own cost and shall fully indemnify PARTY A, the recommended customer and its officers, employees, and agents, against all actions, claims, demands, losses, damages, statutory penalties, expenses, and cost (including legal costs on an indemnity basis), in respect of:

(a)     any and all breach/es of PDPA obligations; or

(b)     any act, omission, or negligence of PARTY B or its subcontractors that causes or results in PARTY A or the customer being in breach of the PDPA.

## 46. Person

Any individual, corporation, partnership, joint venture, limited liability company, estate, trust, unincorporated association, any municipal government or any bureau, department or agency and any fiduciary acting in such capacity on behalf of any of the foregoing.

## 47. Pre-emptive Rights

1. The Company shall give to the Investor ("Pre-emptive Right Holder") a pre-emptive right of subscription ("Pre-emptive Right") in the event that it proposes to undertake any future equity financing during the pendency of this Agreement by an offer for sale of existing Equity Shares or by making a preferential allotment of equity or instruments convertible into shares to third parties (a "Preferential Allotment").

2. The Pre-emptive Right shall be offered by the Company by issuing a written notice on the Pre-emptive Right Holder ("Issuance Notice") setting forth in detail the terms of the proposed issuance, including the proposed issuance price ("Issuance Price"), the date of closing of the proposed issuance (which shall not be less than thirty (30) days from the date of receipt of the Issuance Notice) and the number of Equity Shares or instruments or securities convertible into Equity Shares proposed to be issued ("Issuance Shares").

3. If the Pre-emptive Right Holder wishes to exercise its Pre-emptive Right, within thirty (30) days from the date of receipt of the Issuance Notice, it shall pay for and subscribe to such number of the Issuance Shares as it wish to subscribe to so as to maintain its pro rata holding in the Company as at the time immediately following Closing at the Issuance Price and on the terms and conditions set out in the Issuance Notice. Subject to the receipt of the payment against exercise of the Pre-emptive Right by the Pre-emptive Right Holder, the Company shall issue and allot the Issuance Shares to the Pre-emptive Right Holder on the date of closing of the issuance as stated in the Issuance Notice.

4. If the Pre-emptive Right Holder does not exercise the Pre-emptive Right and make payment to the Company against such exercise within the time period specified in Clause 19.3 above, then the Company may issue and allot the Issuance Shares to a third-party subscriber ("Third Party Subscriber") at the Issuance Price as mentioned in the Issuance Notice.

5.  The Parties hereby agree that there exists no commitment by the Investor to further capitalize the Company or provide finance to the Company in the form, inter alia, of guarantees or loans.

**Comments**

Pre-emptive rights refer to the contractual rights of certain shareholders or partners to purchase additional shares before the company offers them to external parties. Essentially, this provides existing shareholders the opportunity to maintain their proportional ownership in the business when new shares are issued, thereby diluting the voting and economic power of existing shares to a lesser extent than they otherwise would be.

The significant aspects would be control, economic interest, attracting investments, funding, tracking overheads, relationship management, and market effects.

### 48. Put-Call Options

(a) To the extent permitted by Applicable Law and subject to Clause (f) below:

    (i) in the period commencing on the date on which the members of the Y Family cease to Control the X Shareholder (the "Trigger Date") and ending on the date falling one (1) month thereafter ("Put Option Expiry Date"), the PARTY A Shareholder shall have the right (but not the obligation) to demand the X Shareholder to purchase all of the PARTY A Shares, free from all Encumbrances and with all rights and benefits attaching thereto, which the X Shareholder hereby agrees to be obligated to purchase upon such demand, at the price per PARTY A Share as determined based on the Fair Market Value (the "Put Option");

    (ii) if the Put Option is not exercised within the period specified in Clause (a).1, in the period commencing on the Put Option Expiry Date and ending on the date falling one (1) month thereafter, the X Shareholder shall have the right (but not the obligation) to demand the PARTY A Shareholder to sell all of the PARTY A Shares, free from all Encumbrances and with all rights and benefits attaching thereto, which the PARTY A Shareholder hereby agrees to be obligated to sell upon such demand, at the price per PARTY A Share as determined based on the Fair Market Value (the "Call Option").

(b) In case the PARTY A Shareholder intends to exercise its Put Option right under this Clause, it must serve a written notice to the X Shareholder which shall be in the form attached hereto as Schedule 10 (the "Put Exercise Notice").

(c) In case the X Shareholder intends to exercise its Call Option right under this Clause, it must serve a written notice to the PARTY A Shareholder which shall be in the form attached hereto as Schedule 10 (the "Call Exercise Notice").

(d) To the extent permitted by Applicable Law and subject to Clause (f), upon ten (10) Business Days after its receipt of:

   (i)   The Put Exercise Notice and the determination of the Fair Market Value in accordance with Schedule 13, the X Shareholder shall be obligated to purchase the Shares from the PARTY A Shareholder at the price per Share as determined based on the Fair Market Value; or

   (ii)  the Call Exercise Notice and the determination of the Fair Market Value in accordance with Schedule 13, the PARTY A Shareholder shall be obligated to sell the PARTY A Shares to the X Shareholder at the price per PARTY A Share as determined based on the Fair Market Value

(e) The fees and expenses in relation to the sale and purchase of PARTY A Shares under this Clause shall be jointly borne by the PARTY A Shareholder and the X Shareholder.

(f) In the event that the purchase of the PARTY A Shares by the X Shareholder pursuant to the exercise of the Put Option or the Call Option would result in the X Shareholder being in breach of

Applicable Law, any provision of its Constitution or any order, judgment or decree of any court or law or regulation of any governmental authority having jurisdiction over the X Shareholder or any agreement, arrangement or obligation by which the X Shareholder and/or any of its assets or undertakings is bound, the Parties agree that the X Shareholder shall be entitled to nominate a third party purchaser(s) to take up all or some of such PARTY A Shares which the X Shareholder would otherwise be transferred pursuant to the exercise of the Put Option or the Call Option, for compliance with Applicable Law. Should the X Shareholder be unable to find such third-party purchaser(s) within one (1) month of the date of the Put Option Notice or Call Option Notice (as the case may be), the Put Option and the Call Option under this Clause shall immediately lapse, and Parties shall take all such steps as may be necessary to procure the voluntary winding up of the Company. For the avoidance of doubt, the Parties agree and acknowledge that any distribution to the Shareholders upon such voluntary winding up of the Company will be in accordance with Applicable Law and based on their respective equity shareholdings in the Company.

**Comments**

Put Option: Provides the option holder (usually the seller) the right, but not the obligation, to sell a certain asset to the option writer (usually the buyer) at a predetermined price within a certain timeframe. Again, the option holder pays a premium to the option writer for this right.

Call Option: Gives the option holder (usually the buyer) the right, but not the obligation, to buy a certain asset from the option writer (usually the seller) at a predetermined price (the "strike" price) within a specified timeframe. The option holder pays a premium to the option writer for this right.

Put-Call options can help provide price certainty, risk management, and flexibility. There may however be legal and tax implications.

### 49. Related Parties Transaction

(a) In relation to an entity —

    i.    a director or an equivalent person of the entity;

    ii.   the chief executive officer or equivalent person of the entity;

    iii.  a person who controls the entity;

    iv.  a related corporation, i.e., where a corporation —

        (aa) is the holding company of another corporation;

        (bb) is a subsidiary of another corporation; or

        (cc) is a subsidiary of the holding company of another corporation;

    v.   any other entity controlled by it;

    vi.  any other entity controlled by the person referred to in clause iii above; and

    vii. a related party of any individual referred to in clause i, ii or iii above; and

(b) in relation to an individual —

    i.    his immediate family;

    ii.   a trustee of any trust of which the individual or any member of the individual's immediate family is —

        (aa) a beneficiary; or

        (bb) where the trust is a discretionary trust, a discretionary object,

        when the trustee acts in that capacity; and

    iii.  any corporation in which he and his immediate family (whether directly or indirectly) have interests in voting shares of an aggregate of not less than 30% of the total votes attached to all voting shares.

**Comments**

Related party transactions refer to deals or arrangements between two parties who have a pre-existing relationship. In a business context, this usually involves transactions between company and its key management personnel, directors, shareholders, subsidiaries, parent companies, or other affiliates.

Related party transactions can vary widely in nature, including but not

limited to:
- Sales or purchases of goods and services
- Leases
- Transfer of assets or liabilities
- Loans
- Guarantees

### 50. Related Parties (alternate)

Where applicable, means any Person including and not limited to subsidiaries, customers, clients, shareholders, business affiliates, shareholders or shareholder groups, minority owned companies, parties related by way of contract, friends, colleagues and employees and officers of a Party and subordinates thereto. Notwithstanding anything to the contrary and contained herein, the following shall also mean and be deemed to be included as Related Parties.

    (a)    spouse or partner considered to be equivalent to a spouse in accordance with Applicable Law;

    (b)    a dependent child, in accordance with Applicable Law;

    (c)    a relative who has shared the same household for at least one year from the date of the commencement of any agreement between the Recipient with the Company;

    (d)    a legal person, trust or partnership, the managerial responsibilities of which are discharged by a person discharging managerial responsibilities or by a person referred to in point (a), (b) or (c) herein, which is directly or indirectly controlled by such a person, which is set up for the benefit of such a person, or the economic interests of which are substantially equivalent to those of such a person; or

    (e)    a legal entity whose operations a party mentioned above has significant influence over and in which the party mentioned above or someone in (a)-(d) above or them together has such an ownership stake, financial stake or voting stake mentioned in (a) to (d).

### 51. Replacement

This Agreement supersedes all earlier correspondence, understandings and agreements concerning the subject matter hereof.

**Comments**
See Parol Evidence Rule, Entire Agreement, Construction, and Interpretation.

52. Representations and Warranties
1. INFORMATION
    1.1 Information in this Agreement
        The particulars relating to the Company in this Agreement are true and accurate in all respects and are not misleading.
    1.2 Memorandum of Disclosure
        The information contained in the Memorandum of Disclosure and the documents annexed to or referred to in it is true and accurate in all respects and is not misleading, whether because of any omission or ambiguity or for any other reason.
    1.3 Other Information
        All information contained in any document or communication (whether oral or written) which has been given by the Vendor or its Representatives to the Purchaser or its Representatives in the course of the negotiations leading to this Agreement was when given, true and accurate in all respects and is not misleading whether because of any omission or ambiguity or for any other reason. Copies of all contracts and other documents supplied to the Purchaser or any of its Representatives by or on behalf of the Vendor or the Company or any of their respective Representatives are true and complete and the contents of such copy contracts comprise the entire agreement between the parties to them. After making due and careful enquiries, the Vendor is not aware of any fact or matter not Disclosed in writing to the Purchaser which renders any such information untrue, inaccurate, or misleading or the disclosure of which might affect the willingness of the Purchaser to purchase the Sale Shares / subscribe Equity Shares from the Vendor on the terms of this Agreement or the price at or terms upon which the

Purchaser would be willing to purchase them.

2.  CONSTITUTIONAL AND CORPORATE DOCUMENTS
    2.1  Constitutional Documents
    The copies of the memorandum and articles of association or other constitutional and corporate documents of the Company disclosed to the Purchaser or its Representatives are true, accurate and complete in all respects and contain full details of the rights and restrictions attached to the share capital of the Company. Copies of all the resolutions and agreements (including without limitation, shareholders' agreements, voting agreements, etc.) required to be annexed to or incorporated in the constitutive documents of the Company by the law applicable are annexed or incorporated and there have been no amendments to such constitutive documents since the date hereof.
    2.2  Books and Records
    (a)  The statutory records, registers and books and the books of account of the Company have been properly kept, are duly entered up and maintained in accordance with all legal requirements applicable thereto and contain true, full and accurate records of all matters required to be dealt with therein and all such books and all records and documents (including documents of title and copies of all subsisting agreements to which the Company is a party) are its property, in its possession or under its control.
    (b)  The Company has not received any notice of any application or intended application under any applicable legislation for the rectification of its statutory records, registers and/or books.
    2.3  Returns and Filings
    All returns, particulars, resolutions, and other documents which the Company is required by law to file with or deliver to any authority in any jurisdiction [(including the Accounting and Corporate Regulatory Authority of Singapore)] have been correctly made up and filed or, as the case may be, delivered. In particular, all charges in favor of the Company have (if

appropriate) been registered in accordance with the provisions of any applicable legislation.

2.4 Powers of Attorney and Authorities

The Company has not given a power of attorney or other authority by which a person may enter into an agreement, arrangement, or obligation on the Company's behalf (other than an authority for a director, other officer, or employee to enter into an agreement in the usual course of that person's duties).

3. AUDITED ACCOUNTS

3.1 Compliance with Law and Accounting Standards

The Audited Accounts [and/or the Management Accounts] have been prepared in accordance with all applicable laws and accounting standards, policies, principles, and practices generally accepted at the date hereof in the jurisdiction which the Company may be subject to the laws of.

3.2 Auditors

The Audited Accounts have been audited by an auditor or firm of accountants qualified to act as auditors in [Singapore] and the auditors' report(s) required to be annexed to the Accounts is unqualified.

3.3 True and Fair View

The Audited Accounts [and/or the Management Accounts] give a true and fair view of the state of affairs of the Company as at the date of the Audited Accounts [and/or the Management Accounts] and the profits and losses, changes in equity and cash flows of the Company for the relevant financial period.

3.4 Provisions

The Audited Accounts make:

(a) full provision for all actual liabilities;

(b) proper and adequate provision (or note in accordance with good accountancy practice) for all contingent liabilities;

(c) proper and adequate provision or reserve for all bad and doubtful debts; and

(d) due provision for depreciation and amortization and for any obsolescence of assets.

3.5 Stocks

The stock and work-in-progress are included in the Audited Accounts [and/or the Management Accounts] at figures not exceeding the amounts which could, in the circumstances existing at the date of the Audited Accounts [and/or Management Accounts] respectively, reasonably be expected to be realized in the normal course of carrying on the business of the Company.

3.6 Taxation

Full provision or reserve has been made in the Audited Accounts [and/or the Management Accounts] for all Taxation liable to be assessed on the Company or for which it is or may become accountable in respect of:

(a) profits, gains, or income (as computed for Taxation purposes) arising or accruing or deemed to arise or accrue on or before the date of the Audited Accounts [and/or the Management Accounts respectively];

(b) any Transactions effected or deemed to be effected on or before the date of the Audited Accounts [and/or the Management Accounts respectively] or provided for in the Audited Accounts [and/or the Management Accounts];

(c) distributions made or deemed to be made on or before the date of the Audited Accounts [and/or the Management Accounts respectively] or provided for in the Audited Accounts [and/or the Management Accounts]; and

(d) deferred Taxation.

3.7 Profits

The profits and losses of the Company for the financial year ended on the Balance Sheet Date as shown by the Audited Accounts, the audited accounts of the Company for previous periods delivered to the Purchaser [and the Management Accounts] and the trend of profits thereby shown have not (except as therein disclosed) been affected by inconsistencies of accounting practices, by the inclusion of unusual or non-recurring items of income or expenditure, by Transactions entered into otherwise than on normal commercial terms or by any other factors rendering such profits for all or any of such periods exceptionally high or low (other than as disclosed in the relevant accounts).

3.8 Consistent Basis

(a) The Audited Accounts have been prepared on a basis consistent with the audited accounts of the Company for the two (2) preceding financial years without any changes in accounting policies used.

(b) [The Management Accounts have been prepared on a basis consistent with the Audited Accounts and there has been no revaluation of any assets, fixed or otherwise, from the value of those assets stated in the Audited Accounts.]

3.9 Filings

The Audited Accounts have been filed in accordance with the requirements of the Companies Act.

3.10 Transactions Affecting the Accounts

(a) The Company does not have any outstanding loan capital, nor has it factored any of its debts, or engaged in financing of a type which would not be required to be shown or reflected in the Audited Accounts [and/or the Management Accounts] or borrowed any money which it has not repaid (save as disclosed in the relevant accounts).

(b) There are no liabilities (including contingent liabilities) which are outstanding on the part of the Company, other than those liabilities disclosed in the Audited Accounts [and/or the Management Accounts] or which have arisen in the ordinary course of business since the date of the Audited Accounts [and/or the Management Accounts respectively.]

(c) No Transaction of any importance to which the Company has been party has taken place which, if it had taken place on or before the date of the Audited Accounts [or the Management Accounts], would have been required to be disclosed or reflected in the Audited Accounts [or the Management Accounts, as the case may be].

(d) Revenue costs of an occasional or seasonal nature (including any holiday pay, closure and redundancy costs of fixed-term projects or contracts, bonuses, customer rebates, excess use charges under leasing agreements and maintenance, repairs and renewals) were accrued so as to match them as closely as possible to the related income and provided in the Audited Accounts [and/or the Management Accounts] to the extent of the accrual as at the date of the Audited Accounts [and/or the Management Accounts respectively].

(e) No value was attributed in the Audited Accounts [and/or the Management Accounts] to any asset which was not beneficially owned by the Company at the date of the Audited Accounts [or the Management Accounts, as the case may be,] or which in the case of fixed assets, were not in full and exclusive use for the purposes of the Company's business.

4. CHANGES SINCE THE BALANCE SHEET DATE

Since the Balance Sheet Date as regards the Company:

(a) its business has been lawfully carried on in the ordinary course and so as to maintain the same as a going concern;

(b) it has not disposed of any assets or assumed or incurred any liabilities (including contingent liabilities) otherwise than in the ordinary course of carrying on its business;

(c) its business has not been adversely affected by the loss of any important customer or source of supply or by any abnormal factor not affecting similar businesses to a like extent or by any other cause and the Vendor, after making due and careful enquiries, is not aware of any facts which are likely to give rise to any such effects;

(d) no dividend or other distribution has been, or agreed to be, declared, made, or paid to its members except as provided for in the Audited Accounts;

(e) neither its turnover nor its trading position has deteriorated;

(f) no change has been made in the emoluments or other terms of employment of its directors or any of its employees;

(g) it has not borrowed any money or issued any guarantee or created any Encumbrance over any asset other than as disclosed in the Audited Accounts;

(h) no share or loan capital has been allotted, issued, repaid, or redeemed and no agreement or arrangement has been made to do any of the foregoing;

(i) there has been no unusual increase or decrease in the level of its stock;

(j) it has not entered into any unusual, long term or onerous commitments or contracts;

(k) after making due and careful enquiries, it has not learnt of any circumstance making bad or doubtful any of its book debts;

(l) there has been no material adverse change in its business, operations, assets, financial condition or prospects and no event, fact or matter has occurred or is likely to occur which will or is likely to give rise to any such change;

(m) it has not knowingly waived or released any proprietary rights howsoever arising;

(n) it has not acquired or disposed of or granted any right or option or created any other Encumbrance, save for those created pursuant to this Agreement;

(o) no resolution has been passed and nothing has been done in the conduct or management of the affairs of the Company which would be likely to reduce the net asset value of the Company;

(p) no change has been made to the accounting practices adopted in relation to the Company and the accounting practices adopted for the Company are consistent with those adopted in the Audited Accounts;

(q) it has not changed its accounting reference period; and

(r) no claim sounding in damages has been made against the Company.

5. TAXATION

5.1 General

(a)     The Company is and has at all times been resident only in [Singapore] for all Taxation purposes. The Company is not liable to pay and has at no time incurred any liability to Taxation chargeable under the laws of any jurisdiction other than [Singapore].

(b)     without prejudice to any other provision of this Agreement, there is no liability to Taxation in respect of, as a result of or in consequence of any Claim for Taxation which has been made or may hereafter be made:

  i)      in respect of or arising from any Transaction effected or deemed to have been effected on or before Completion; or

  ii)     by reference to any income, profits or gains earned, accrued, or received on or before Completion,

except:

to the extent that provision or reserve specifically in respect thereof was made in the Audited Accounts;

(aa)    in respect of Taxation attributable to Transactions arising out of the ordinary course of the normal trading of the Company; and

(bb)    to the extent that such Claim arises as a result only of any provision or reserve in respect thereof being insufficient by reason of any increase in rates of Taxation made after the date hereof with retrospective effect, and there are no circumstances likely to give rise to such a liability.

(cc)    The Company is not and will not become, liable to pay, or make reimbursement or indemnity in respect of, any Taxation (or amounts corresponding thereto) as a consequence of the failure by any other person to discharge that Taxation within any specified period or otherwise, where such Taxation relates to a profit, income or gain, transaction, event, omission or circumstance arising, occurring or deemed to arise or occur (whether wholly or partly) prior to Completion.

(dd)    No relief (whether by way of deduction, reduction, set-off, exemption, postponement, roll-over, repayment, or allowance or otherwise) from, against or in respect of any Taxation has been claimed and/or given to the Company which could or might be effectively withdrawn, postponed, restricted, clawed back or otherwise lost as a result of any act, omission, event, or circumstance arising or occurring prior to or on Completion.

(ee)    The Company has not been required by the relevant authorities of customs and excise to give security.

5.2    Tax Returns, Information and Clearances

(a)    All returns, accounts, computations, notices and information which are or have been required to be made, given or delivered by the Company for any Taxation purpose (i) have been made, given or delivered within the requisite periods or within permitted extensions of such periods, (ii) are up-to-date, complete and accurate and made on a proper basis and (iii) none of them is, or is likely to be, the subject of any dispute with the Taxation Authority.

(b)    No Transaction has been effected since the Balance Sheet Date by the Company in respect of which any consent or clearance from the Taxation Authority was or will be required or was or could have been sought (i) without such consent or clearance having been validly obtained before the Transaction was effected, (ii) otherwise than in accordance with the terms of and so as to satisfy any conditions attached to such consent or clearance and (iii) otherwise than at a time when and in circumstances in which such consent or clearance was and will be valid and effective.

(c)    All particulars furnished to the Taxation Authority in connection with any application for consent or clearance by the Company since the Balance Sheet Date fully and accurately disclosed all facts and circumstances material to the decision of the Taxation Authority.

(d)　There are no circumstances that have arisen since the making of any application for any such consent or clearance which might reasonably be expected to cause such consent or clearance to be or become invalid or to be withdrawn by the Taxation Authority.

(e)　The Company has not since the Balance Sheet Date taken any action which has had, or will have, the result of altering, prejudicing or in any way disturbing any arrangement or agreement between the Company and the Taxation Authority.

5.3　Payment of Taxes

(a)　All Taxes assessed or imposed by any government or governmental or statutory body which have been assessed upon the Company and which are due and payable on or before Completion have been paid and were paid on or before the relevant due date for payment.

(b)　There is no further liability or contingent liability for Taxation otherwise than as a result of trading activities in the ordinary course of the Company's business from the Balance Sheet Date.

5.4　Deductions from Payments

(a)　The Company has made all deductions and withholdings in respect or on account of Taxation which it is required or entitled by any relevant legislation to make from any payments made by it including, but not limited to, interest, annuities or other annual payments, royalties, rent, remuneration, payments to employees or sub-contractors or payments to a non-resident and each has accounted in full to the relevant Taxation Authority for any Taxation so deducted or withheld.

(b)　Proper records have been maintained in respect of all such deductions and withholdings and all regulations applicable thereto have been complied with.

5.5 Arm's Length Dealings

(a) The Company does not own, and has not agreed to acquire, any asset, and has not received or agreed to receive any services or facilities (including without limitation, the benefit of any licences or agreements), the consideration for the acquisition or provision of which was or will be in excess of its market value, or otherwise than on an arm's length basis.

(b) The Company has not disposed, or agreed to dispose, of any assets, and has not provided or agreed to provide any services or facilities (including without limitation, the benefit of any licences) which was or will be less than its market value, or otherwise than on an arm's length basis.

(c) The Company has not incurred a loss on the disposal or deemed disposal of an asset other than trading stock in relation to which its ability to set the whole of that loss against any chargeable gain arising in the same or a later accounting period is or may be restricted or excluded.

(d) No asset owned by the Company has at any time since its acquisition been subject to a reduction in value such that any allowable loss arising on its disposal is likely to be reduced or eliminated or any chargeable gain arising on its disposal is likely to be increased.

5.6 Penalties and Interest

Neither the Company nor any of its directors or officers has paid, or become liable to pay, any fine, penalty or interest charged by virtue of any other statutory provision relating to Taxation.

5.7 Anti-avoidance Provision

(a) The Company has not since the Balance Sheet Date engaged in, or been a party to, any Transaction or series of Transactions or scheme or arrangement of which the main purpose, or one of the main purposes, was or could be said to be the avoidance of, or deferral of or a reduction in the liability to, Taxation.

(b)    The Company has not been the subject of an investigation, discovery, or access order by or involving any Taxation Authority and there are no circumstances existing which make it likely that an investigation, discovery, or order will be made.

5.8    Goods and Services Tax ("GST")
(a)    The Company is a taxable person and is duly registered for the purposes of GST with quarterly prescribed accounting periods.
(b)    The Company has complied with all statutory provisions, rules, regulations, orders, requirements, conditions, and directions in respect of GST.
(c)    All supplies made by the Company are taxable supplies and the Company has not been (and will not be) denied full credit for all input tax for any reason. All GST paid (or payable) by the Company is in the form of input tax.
(d)    The Company is not and has not been for GST purposes a member of any group of companies and no act or transaction has been effected in consequence whereof the Company is (or may be) held liable for any GST arising from supplies made by another company.
(e)    The Company maintains complete, correct and up to date records as is required by the applicable legislation.]

5.9    Stamp Duty
(a)    In relation to stamp duty assessable or payable in Singapore or elsewhere in the world, all documents the enforcement of which the Company may be interested have been duly stamped and no document belonging to the Company now or at Completion which is subject to stamp duty is or will be unstamped or insufficiently stamped.
(b)    No relief from stamp duty has been improperly obtained, nor has any event occurred as a result of which any such duty from which the Company has obtained relief has become payable.
(c)    All stamp duty payable upon any transfer of shares in the

Company before Completion has been duly paid.

(d) Neither the entering into of this Agreement nor Completion will affect or result in the withdrawal of any stamp duty relief granted to the Company on or before Completion.

6. EMPLOYEES
6.1 General

(a) The names of each person who is a director or shadow director of the Company are set out in the Memorandum of Disclosure.

(b) The Memorandum of Disclosure lists all individuals who are providing services to the Company under an agreement which is not a contract of employment with the Company (including where the individual acts as a consultant or is on secondment from another company) and the particulars of the terms on which the individual provides services, including:

i. the individual's name;

ii. the remuneration of the individual (including any benefits and privileges provided or which the Company is bound to provide);

iii. the length of notice necessary to terminate the agreement;

iv. the term of the agreement;

v. the country in which the individual provides services, if the individual provides services wholly or mainly outside Singapore; and

vi. the law governing the agreement if the individual provides services wholly or mainly outside Singapore.

(c) Every employee who requires an employment pass or other required permit to work in Singapore has a current employment pass or such other required permit and all necessary permission to remain in Singapore and true and complete particulars of each such employee's current remuneration, age, sex, date of commencement of continuous employment and pension scheme membership are set out in the Memorandum of Disclosure.

(d) The acquisition of the Sale Shares by the Purchaser or compliance with the terms of this Agreement will not enable any directors, officers, or senior employees of the Company to terminate their employment or receive any payment or other benefit.

(e) The Company has not hired or committed to hire any employees or independent contractors or promoted or committed to promoting any employees into or within the director, manager, or officer levels.

(f) There is no agreement, arbitration, or court decisions or governmental, regulatory, or supervisory orders which are binding on the Company which limit or restrict in any way the Company from relocating or closing any of its operations.

6.2 Termination of Employment

(a) No notice to terminate the contract of employment of any employee of the Company (whether given by the Company or by the employee) is pending, outstanding or threatened and no dispute under any Employment Legislation or otherwise is outstanding between the Company and any of its current or former employees relating to their employment, its termination and any reference given by the Company regarding them.

(b) There are not in existence any contracts of service with its employees of the Company, nor any consultancy agreements with the Company, which cannot be terminated by three (3) months' notice or less or (where not reduced to writing) by reasonable notice without giving rise to any claim for damages or compensation.

(c) None of the employees of the Company has tendered to the Company his or her resignation or has otherwise indicated to the Company his or her intention to leave the employment of the Company.

6.3 Remuneration

(a) There are no amounts owing to any present or former directors or to employees of the Company save for accrued benefits and remuneration due to present directors and employees of the Company, full details of which have been set out in the Audited Accounts [and/or Management Accounts].

(b) Save to the extent (if any) to which provision or allowance has been made in the Audited Accounts [and/or the Management Accounts], the Company has not made nor agreed to make any payment to or provided or agreed to provide any benefit for any present or former director or employee which is not allowable as a deduction for the purposes of Taxation.

(c) Save to the extent (if any) to which provision or allowance has been made in the Audited Accounts [and/or the Management Accounts]:

(i) no liability has been incurred by the Company for breach of any contract of service or for services, for redundancy payments or for compensation for wrongful dismissal or unfair dismissal or for failure to comply with any order for the reinstatement or re-engagement of any employee; and

(ii) no gratuitous payment has been made or promised by the Company in connection with the actual or proposed termination or suspension of employment or variation of any contract of employment of any present or former director or employee.

(d) No employee of the Company is entitled (contingently or otherwise) to receive any bonus, commission, variable remuneration, insurance benefit in kind, motor vehicle for private use or other reward other than wages or salary at a fixed rate.

(e) The Company has not offered nor agreed to increase the remuneration of or to alter any of the terms and conditions of employment of any of its employees.

(f) There are no amounts owing to any present or former employee of the Company other than remuneration accrued for the current wage or salary period or for reimbursement of normal business expenses and no present or former employee of the Company has any claim against the Company or right to be indemnified by the Company arising out of an act or omission in the course of his office or employment on or before the date of this Agreement.

(g) None of the employees of the Company has at the date of this Agreement any accrued rights to holiday pay or to pay in lieu of holidays which have not been provided for in full in the Audited Accounts [and/or Management Accounts].

6.4　Compliance with Law

The Company has in relation to each of its employees (and so far, as relevant to each of its former employees) complied in all respects with:

(a) all obligations imposed on it by all statutes, regulations and codes of conduct and practice relevant to the relations between it and its employees or any trade union and has maintained current, adequate, and suitable records regarding the service of each of its employees;

(b) all collective agreements and customs and practices for the time being dealing with such relations or the conditions of service of its employees;

(c) all relevant orders and awards made under any relevant statute, regulation or code of conduct and practice affecting the conditions of service of its employees; and

(d) all obligations under statute or otherwise concerning the health and safety at work of its employees, and there are no claims pending or threatened, or capable of arising, against the Company by a present or former employee or third party, in respect of an accident or injury which is not fully covered by insurance.

6.5　Trade Unions and Industrial Relations

(a) The Company is not involved in, nor has it received notice of any industrial or trade dispute or any dispute or negotiation with any trade union or association of trade unions or organisation or body of employees and there is nothing likely to give rise to such a dispute or claim.

(b) Particulars of all workforce agreements reached under any Employment Legislation and all collective bargaining or procedural or other agreements or arrangements with any trade union, group or organisation representing employees that relate to any employees of the Company are set out in the Memorandum of Disclosure.

(c) There has been no strike, work to rule, work stoppage, work interference activity or industrial action (official or unofficial) by any employee of the Company within the last five (5) years, threatened or otherwise.

6.6 Grants and Employment Schemes

(a) The Company does not have in existence, nor is proposing or bound to introduce, any incentive scheme, share incentive scheme, share option scheme, profit sharing scheme or other bonus commission or incentive scheme for all or any part of its directors or employees.

(b) There is not in existence nor has any proposal been announced to establish any retirement, death or disability benefit schemes for directors or employees nor are there any obligations to or in respect of present or former directors or employees with regard to retirement, death or disability pursuant to which the Company is or may become liable to make payments and no pension or retirement or sickness gratuity is currently being paid or has been promised by the Company to or in respect of any former director or former employee.

(c) No grants, subsidies or allowances have been applied for or received by the Company from any government body and there are no grounds upon which any such grant, subsidy or allowance or any part thereof could be liable to be repaid or recovered whether by reason of completion of this Agreement or otherwise.

(d) The Company is not party to any scheme or programme relating to the temporary or permanent engagement or training of employees under which it receives any subsidy or other financial assistance from any government body.

6.7   Central Provident Fund Contributions
All deductions and payments required to be made by the
Company in respect of Central Provident Fund contributions
(including employer's contributions) in relation to the
remuneration of the employees (if applicable) to any relevant
competent authority have been so made.

6.8   Retirement Benefits
[EITHER:
There is no arrangement under which the Company has or may
    have any obligation (whether or not legally binding) to
    provide or contribute towards pension, lump sum, death, ill-
    health, disability or accident benefits in respect of its past or
    present officers and employees and no proposal or
    announcement has been made to any employee or officer of
    the Company about the introduction, continuance, increase
    or improvement of, or the payment of a contribution
    towards, any other pension, lump sum, death, ill-health,
    disability or accident benefit.
OR:
(a) The pension scheme known as the "[_____]" ("Pension
    Scheme") is the only arrangement under which the Company
    has or may have any obligation (whether or not legally
    binding) to provide or contribute towards pension, lump sum,
    death, ill-health, disability or accident benefits in respect of
    its past or present officers and employees ("Pensionable
    Employees") and no proposal or announcement has been
    made to any employee or officer of the Company about the
    introduction, continuance, increase or improvement of, or
    the payment of a contribution towards, any other pension,
    lump sum, death, ill-health, disability or accident benefit.
(b) The Memorandum of Disclosure sets out a list of all
    Pensionable Employees who are members of the Pension
    Scheme with all details relevant to their membership and
    necessary to establish their entitlements under the Pension

Scheme.

(c) All contributions and deductions due to and in respect of the Pension Scheme have been duly paid and there are no liabilities outstanding in respect of the Pension Scheme as at the date of this Agreement.

(d) No discrimination on grounds of sex is, or has at any stage been, made in the provision of pension, lump sum, death, ill-health, disability, or accident benefits by the Company in relation to any of the Pensionable Employees.

(e) No claims or complaints have been made or are pending or threatened in relation to the Pension Scheme or in respect of the provision of (or failure to provide) pension, lump sum, death, ill-health, disability, or accident benefits by the Company in relation to any of the Pensionable Employees and there is no fact or circumstance likely to give rise to such claims or complaints.]

7.  DEBTS TO, AND CONTRACTS WITH, CONNECTED PERSONS
    (a) There are:
    - (i) no loans made by the Company to, and (B) no debts (whether or not due for payment and including contingent liabilities) other than debts which have arisen in the ordinary course of business or unfulfilled obligations (present or future, actual or contingent) owing by the Company to, the Vendor or to any director, officer, employee or shareholder of the Company or any person Connected to any of them;
    - (ii) no debts owing by the Company other than debts which have arisen in the ordinary course of business;
    - (iii) no securities given by or to the Company (including guarantees or indemnities) for any such loans or debts as aforesaid; and
    - (iv) no claim or circumstance which may give rise to a claim against the Company by the Vendor or any director, officer, employee or shareholder of the Company or any person Connected to any of them.
    (b) There are no existing contracts, arrangements,

understandings, or engagements to which the Company is a party and in which the Vendor and/or any director, officer, employee, or shareholder of the Company and/or any person connected to any of them is directly or indirectly interested.

(c) There is no contract, arrangement or understanding to which the Company is a party or by which it is bound, which is not on entirely arm's length terms.

(d) The financial position of the Company and its results as appearing from the Audited Accounts [and/or the Management Accounts] were not and have not since been affected by any Transaction, contract, or arrangement not entirely on arm's length terms.

(e) None of the Vendor, director, officer, employee or shareholder of the Company or any person Connected to any of them is entitled to a claim of any nature against the Company or has assigned to any person the benefit of a claim against the Company to which the Vendor, any director, officer, employee or shareholder of the Company or a person Connected to any of them would otherwise be entitled.

8.  BANKING AND FINANCE

8.1 Borrowings

(a) Save as disclosed in the Audited Accounts or the Memorandum of Disclosure, the Company does not have outstanding, and has not agreed to create or incur, loan capital, borrowings, or indebtedness in the nature of borrowings.

(b) The total borrowings of the Company does not exceed any limitations on its borrowing powers contained in the memorandum and articles of association of the Company or in any debenture or other deed or document binding on the Company.

(c) The Company is not a party to any loan agreement, facility letter or other agreement for the provision of credit or financing facilities to it or any agreement for the sale, factoring or discounting of debts.

(d) The Company has not engaged in any borrowing or financing

Transaction or arrangement which does not appear as borrowings in the Audited Accounts.

(e)   All of the Company's borrowings may be repaid by it at any time at no more than one (1) months' notice and without any premium or penalty (howsoever called) on repayment.

(f)   The Company has not lent any money that has not been repaid and there are no debts owing to the Company other than debts that have arisen in the normal course of business.

(g)   The debts owing to the Company shown in the Audited Accounts [and the Management Accounts] were paid in full on the date they became due (except for any provision for bad or doubtful debts made in the Audited Accounts [and the Management Accounts]).

(h)   All other debts owing to the Company are or will be recoverable in full as and when they fall due.

(i)   The Company shall be free of any debt or liability of any nature whatsoever (whether actual, contingent, or otherwise) as at the Completion Date [other than debts that have arisen in the normal course of business].

8.2  Guarantees and Indemnities

(a)   Neither the Company nor any other person has given or entered into or undertaken to give or enter into any guarantee, Encumbrances or other security agreement or arrangement for any of the Company's liability (contingent or otherwise), borrowings or other obligations.

(b)   The Company has not given or entered into or undertaken to give or enter into any guarantee, Encumbrances or other security agreement or arrangement for the liability, borrowings or other obligations of any person and the Company is not responsible for the indebtedness or the default in performance of any person.

8.3  Events of Default

No event has occurred or been alleged to have occurred and no circumstances have arisen which:

(a) constitutes an event of default, or otherwise gives rise to an obligation to repay (prematurely or otherwise), under an agreement relating to borrowing or indebtedness in the nature of borrowing (or will do so with the giving of notice or lapse of time or both);

(b) will lead to an Encumbrance constituted or created in connection with borrowing or indebtedness in the nature of borrowing, a guarantee, an indemnity, or other obligation of the Company becoming enforceable (or will do so with the giving of notice or lapse of time or both);

(c) would entitle a provider of finance to the Company (other than on a normal overdraft facility) to call in the whole or any part of the monies advanced or to enforce its security (or will do so with the giving of notice or lapse of time or both); and

(d) would entitle a provider of finance to the Company to withdraw, reduce or not renew any existing facilities to the Company or alter any terms thereof to the Company's disadvantage.

8.4 General

(a) Save as disclosed in the Memorandum of Disclosure, the Company does not have any bank, building society or other similar account (whether in credit or overdrawn). Full details of all bank accounts of the Company, including the overdraft limits, bank balances and copies of the relevant bank mandates are set out in the Memorandum of Disclosure. There has been no payments out of or drawings against the said account(s) except for payments in the ordinary and proper course of business.

(b) The Company is not subject to any arrangement for receipt or repayment of any grant, subsidy or financial assistance from any government department or other body.

(c) Having regard to the existing banking and other facilities available to it, the Company has sufficient working capital for the purposes of:

(i) continuing to carry on its business in its present form and at its present level of turnover; and

  (ii) executing, carrying out and fulfilling in accordance with their respective terms all orders, projects and contractual obligations which have been placed with or undertaken by the Company.

 (d) The change in the shareholdings of the Company upon Completion will not:

  (i) result in the termination of or materially affect any financial agreement or arrangement to which the Company is a party or subject; or

  (ii) result in any indebtedness of the Company becoming due, or capable of being declared due and payable, prior to its stated maturity.

9. BOOK DEBTS

Save as disclosed in the Audited Accounts [and/or the Management Accounts], none of the book debts which are included in the Audited Accounts or which have arisen after the Balance Sheet Date have been outstanding for more than three (3) months from their due dates for payment and each such debt has realized or will realize in the normal course of collection its full value as included in the Audited Accounts or in the books of the Company after taking into account any provision for such debt made in the Audited Accounts.

10. CONTRACTS

10.1 General

 (a) None of the contracts or purported contracts of the Company is void, voidable or unenforceable by it. The Company is not in breach of any of its contractual obligations and [and so far as the Vendor is aware,] no other party to any contract to which the Company is a party is in breach of that contract or is unlikely to be able or willing to fulfil its contractual obligations. The expression "so far as the Vendor is aware" shall be deemed to refer to the knowledge of the Vendor after having made all reasonable endeavors to ensure that all information given, referred to or reflected in this statement is accurate in all material aspects.

(b) No event or omission has occurred or been permitted to arise which would entitle any third party to terminate prematurely any contract to which the Company is a party or call in any money or enforce any obligation before the date on which payment or performance would normally be due.

(c) The Company has completed accurate records of the terms of all contracts to which it is a party or by which it is bound.

10.2  Material Contracts

(a)  The Material Contracts entered into by the Company are listed in the Memorandum of Disclosure.

(b)  No notice of termination of a Material Contract has been received or served by the Company and there are no grounds for determination, rescission, avoidance, repudiation, or a material change in the terms of any such contract.

(c)  True and complete copies of all Material Contracts have been delivered by the Vendor to the Purchaser.

10.3  Long Term and Other Onerous Contracts

(a) The Company is not a party to or subject to any agreement or arrangement which:

(i)  is of an unusual or exceptional nature;

(ii) is entered into otherwise than in the ordinary and usual course of business of the Company;

(iii) may be terminated as a result of any change in shareholding in the Company;

(iv) restricts the freedom of the Company to carry on the whole or any part of its business in any part of the world in such manner as it thinks fit;

(v) is of an onerous or long-term nature; and

(vi) is or may become terminable or which contain provisions which may operate adversely against the Company as a result of the entry into or completion of this Agreement.

(b)  The Company:

(i)  is not nor has it agreed to become a member of any joint venture, consortium, partnership or other unincorporated association or a party to any agreement or arrangement for participating with others in any business sharing commissions or other income;

(ii) is not nor has it agreed to become a party to any agency, distributorship, marketing, purchasing, manufacturing, or licensing agreement or arrangement or any agreement or arrangement of any nature whatsoever which restricts its freedom to carry on its business in any part of the world in any manner; and

(iii) has not sold nor will it at any time prior to Completion sell or otherwise dispose of any shares or capital or assets in circumstances such that it is, or may be, still subject to any liability (whether contingent or otherwise) under any representation, warranty or indemnity given or agreed to be given on or in connection with such sale or disposal.

10.4 Compliance

(a) The terms of all leases, tenancies, licenses, concessions, agencies, franchises, and agreements of whatsoever nature to which the Company is a party have been duly complied with by it.

(b) No such lease, tenancy, licence, concession, agency, franchise, or agreement will become subject to avoidance, revocation or be otherwise affected upon or in consequence of the making or implementation of this Agreement.

## 11. INSURANCE

11.1 Insurance of Assets:

Each insurable asset of the Company has at all times been and is at the date of this Agreement insured to its full replacement value (with no provision for deduction or excess) or reinstatement value against fire and other risks normally insured against by persons operating the types of businesses operated by the Company.

11.2 Other Insurances:

The Company has at all times been and is at the date of this

Agreement adequately insured against accident, damage, injury, third party loss (including without limitation, product liability), credit risk, loss of profits and all other risks to persons operating the types of businesses operated by the Company is exposed.

11.3    Policies;
The following information in relation to each of the Policies has been Disclosed in the Memorandum of Disclosure and such information is true and accurate in all respects:
(a)     name of insured(s);
(b)     name of insurer(s);
(c)     period of cover;
(d)     classes of risks covered;
(e)     basis of cover (i.e., claims made or losses occurring);
(f)     deductibility (amount deductible and details of whether it is applied on (A) a per "cause" or "event" basis, and/or (B) an aggregate basis);
(g)     any applicable limits (including any per "cause" or "event" limits and any aggregate limits);
(h)     the premium payable in respect of the Policy;
(i)     all exclusions contained in the Policy; and
(j)     any relevant conditions or warranties which may affect the availability of cover under the Policy.

11.4    Status of Policies
(a)     Each of the Policies is valid and enforceable and is not void or voidable.
(b)     The Company has not done anything or omitted to do anything which might:
(i)     make any of the Policies void or voidable; or
(ii)    prejudice the ability to effect insurance on the same or better terms in the future.
(c)     No insurer under any of the Policies has disputed, or given any indication that they intend to dispute, the validity of any of the Policies on any grounds.
(d)     There is nothing which could:

      (i)       vitiate any of the Policies; or

      (ii)      prejudice the ability to effect insurance on the same or better terms in the future.

(e)      None of the Policies contains any provisions as to the change of control or ownership of the insured.

(f)      No insurer has ever cancelled or refused to accept or continue any insurance in relation to the Company.

**11.5     Premiums**

In respect of all Policies:

(a)      all premiums have been duly paid to date;

(b)      none of the Policies is subject to any special or unusual terms or restrictions or to the payment of any premium in excess of the usual rate; and

(c)      the Company has not done anything or omitted to do anything, and there is nothing, which might result in an increase in the premium payable under any of the Policies.

**11.6     Claims**

(a)      No claims have been made or are outstanding in respect of, and no fact or circumstance exists which might give rise to a claim under, any of the Policies.

(b)      No event, act or omission has occurred which requires notification under any of the Policies.

(c)      None of the insurers under any of the Policies has refused, or given any indication that it intends to refuse, indemnity in whole or in part in respect of any claims under the Policies.

(d)      Nothing has been done or omitted to be done, and there is nothing, which might entitle the insurers under any of the Policies to refuse indemnity in whole or in part in respect of any claims under the Policies.

## 12. ASSETS

**12.1     Title**

(a) All assets (including all intangible assets) owned, held, or used by and all debts due to the Company which are included in the Audited Accounts [and/or the Management Accounts] or Memorandum of Disclosure or have otherwise been represented as being the property of and due to the Company:

(b) are legally and beneficially owned by it free from any Encumbrance;

(i) are in its possession or under its exclusive control; and

(ii) are situated in its country of incorporation.

(c) There is no Encumbrance on, over or affecting the whole or any part of the undertaking, assets, or debts of the Company (including, where appropriate, its investment in its subsidiaries or associated companies) and there is no agreement or commitment to give or create any Encumbrance and no claim has been made by any person to be entitled to any Encumbrance.

(d) The Company has good and marketable title to all the assets owned by it.

(e) The assets owned by the Company comprise all the assets necessary to enable the Company to carry on its business fully and effectively in the ordinary course as carried on up to and as at the date of this Agreement and no such assets are used wholly or partly for any purpose other than the Company's business.

(f) All assets owned or used by the Company which are subject to a requirement of licensing or registration of ownership, possession or use are duly licensed or registered in its sole name. In particular, all vehicles owned or used by the Company (including without limitation, company vehicles used by any of its employees) are registered in its sole name and are duly licensed and insured for all purposes for which they are used, all registration documents relating thereto are in its possession, and all necessary goods vehicle operators' licences are held by it.

(g)     The assets registers of the Company comprise a complete and accurate record of all plant, machinery, equipment, vehicles, and other assets owned, held, or used by it and are capable of being reconciled in respect of each item with the book values of such assets in its accounting records.

(h)     The Company has not received any sum, property or benefit the payment or transfer of which is liable to be avoided, or which is liable to be recovered from it, under any rule or law and does not hold any sum, property or right as trustee or constructive trustee.

12.2     Hire Purchase and Leased Assets

(a)     [Save as Disclosed in the Memorandum of Disclosure,] none of the undertaking, assets or debts of the Company is the subject of any factoring arrangement, hire-purchase, lease, lease hire, licence, conditional sale or credit sale agreement or agreement for payment on deferred terms.

(b)     [Nothing has occurred or is likely to occur in relation to an asset held by the Company under a lease or similar agreement, whereby the rental payable has been, or is likely to be, increased.]

12.3     Condition

(a)     All plant, machinery, equipment, and vehicles owned or used by the Company are in good and safe repair and condition having regard to their respective age, have been regularly and properly maintained, are suitable for the purposes for which they are used and intended and are in working order, and none is in a dangerous or (in the case of vehicles) unroadworthy condition or in need of renewal or replacement.

(b)     All maintenance contracts (i) in respect of assets of the Company which it is normal or prudent to have maintained by independent or specialist contractors and (ii) in respect of all assets which it is obliged to maintain or repair under any hire purchase, leasing, rental, insurance, or other agreement, are in full force and effect.

12.4 Capital Commitment
The Company does not have any capital commitment [in excess of US$[_____].
Stock
(a) The Company's stock is of satisfactory quality and saleable in the usual course of its business in accordance with its current price list.
(b) The Company has not supplied, or agreed to supply, defective or unsafe goods or goods which fail to comply with their terms of sale.
(c) No goods in a state ready for supply by the Company are defective or unsafe or will fail to comply with terms of sale similar to terms of sale on which similar goods have previously been sold by the Company.
(d) The Company's level of stock is reasonable having regard to current and anticipated demand.

13. INTELLECTUAL PROPERTY RIGHTS
13.1 Ownership
(a) Each of the Intellectual Property Rights used or required by the Company in connection with its business (including without limitation, all and any products manufactured, assembled and/or sold or leased or rented by it) is:
(i) in full force and effect and valid and enforceable and nothing has been done or omitted to be done by which it may cease to be valid and enforceable;
(ii) legally and beneficially owned by, vested in,

and validly granted to, the Company alone, free from any licence, Encumbrance, restriction on use or disclosure obligation; and

(iii) not, and will not be, the subject of a claim or opposition from a person (including without limitation, an employee of the Company) as to title, validity, enforceability, entitlement or otherwise.

(b) Without prejudice to paragraph 13.1(a) above, the Company has copyright in all drawings and design rights in all designs relating to its business and all such drawings and designs are in its possession and it has not supplied copies of any such drawings or designs to any other person.

(c) The Intellectual Property Rights as set out in the Memorandum of Disclosure comprise all the Intellectual Property Rights used or required by the Company in connection with its business as it has been operated before the date of this Agreement. The Company does not require any patent, trade or service mark, registered design, copyright, design right, licence, or other right of any other person in order to manufacture or sell or lease its products or to use the processes employed in its business as presently carried on.

(d) The Company is the sole beneficial owner of the Intellectual Property Rights listed in the Memorandum of Disclosure and (where registration is possible) it has been and is registered as the proprietor in the territories listed in the Memorandum of Disclosure, and none of them is being used, claimed, opposed, or attached by any other person.

(e) The activities, processes, methods, services, or Intellectual Property Rights used, dealt in, or supplied on or before the date of this Agreement by the Company:

(i)  are not at the date of this Agreement, nor were they at the time used, dealt in, or supplied, subject to the licence, consent, or permission of, or payment to, another person;

(ii)  do not at the date of this Agreement, nor did they at the time used, dealt in, or supplied, infringe, misuse, or embody the subject matter of any rights in the Intellectual Property Rights of another person; and

(iii)  have not given, and will not give, rise to a claim against the Company.

(f)  The Company has not granted and is not obliged to grant a licence, assignment, consent, undertaking, security interest or other right in respect of any of the Intellectual Property Rights listed in the Memorandum of Disclosure.

13.2  Claims and Infringement

(a)  No right or licence has been granted to any person by the Company to use in any manner or to do anything which would or might otherwise infringe any of the Intellectual Property Rights referred to above.

(b)  None of the activities of the Company infringes any patent or other intellectual property of any kind whatsoever of any other person or gives rise to an obligation to pay any sum in the nature of a royalty.

(c)  The business (including without limitation, all and any products manufactured, assembled and/or sold or leased or rented by it) of the Company (and of any licensee under a licence granted by the Company) as now carried on does not and is not likely to infringe any Intellectual Property Right of any other person (or would not do so if the same were valid) or give rise to a liability pursuant to intellectual property laws.

(d)     No party to an agreement relating to the use:

(i)     by the Company of Intellectual Property Rights owned by another person; or

(ii)    of any Intellectual Property Rights owned by the Company by another person,

(e)     is, or has at any time been, in breach of the agreement and no circumstances exist which would give rise to any breach of any such agreement or to any such agreement being terminated, suspended, varied, or revoked without the Company's consent (other than termination without cause upon notice in accordance with the terms of the agreement). All such agreements are in full force and effect and there is not, and never has been, an infringement of or unauthorised use by a party to such agreement of any Intellectual Property Right which is the subject matter of such agreement.

(f)     There is, and for the two (2) years prior to the date of this Agreement has been, no civil, criminal, arbitration or other proceeding or dispute in any jurisdiction concerning any of the Intellectual Property Rights. No such proceeding or dispute is pending or threatened and no fact or circumstance exist which might give rise to a proceeding of that type.

13.3    Confidentiality

(a)     The Company has not (otherwise than in the ordinary and normal course of business) disclosed or permitted to be disclosed or undertaken or arranged to disclose to any person other than the Purchaser any of its know-how, trade secrets, confidential information, price lists or lists of customers or suppliers.

(b)     The Company is not subject to any secrecy

arrangement or agreement and is not otherwise subject to any duty which may restrict the use or disclosure of information.

(c)     All Confidential Information is adequately and properly documented to enable the Purchaser to acquire and retain its full benefit.

13.4    Validity of Agreements

(a)     Nothing has been done or omitted to be done and no circumstance exist by which a person is or will be able to seek cancellation, termination, rectification, or other modification of a registration of, or any licence, agreement or arrangement relating to, any Intellectual Property Rights.

(b)     Nothing has been done or omitted to be done by the Company which in any way constitutes a breach of the terms of any licence, agreement or arrangement relating to any Intellectual Property Rights granted by or to it.

13.5    Renewal and Maintenance Fees

All renewal and maintenance fees and taxes due and payable prior to Completion in respect of each pending and registered Intellectual Property Rights have been paid in full. Other action required to maintain and protect the pending and registered Intellectual Property Rights has been taken.

14. PROPERTY

14.1    Extent of Property

The Property comprises all of the land and buildings owned, vested in, used, or occupied by or in the possession of, the Company. The information relating to the Property set out in [•] is complete and accurate and includes all information needed to identify the Property and its present use.

14.2    Ownership and Title
    (a)    The Company is the legal and beneficial owner of, and is entitled to and has exclusive possession of, the Property.

    (b)    The Company has a good and marketable title to the Property.

    (c)    The Property which is occupied or otherwise used by the Company in connection with its businesses is occupied or used by right of ownership or under lease or licence, the terms of which permit the occupation or use.

    (d)    The information set out in the Memorandum of Disclosure as to the tenure of the Property, the principal terms of the leases or licences held by the Company, and the principal terms of the tenancies and licences subject to and with the benefit of which the Property is held is accurate and complete in all respects.

    (e)    The Company has no right of ownership, right of use, option, right of first refusal or contractual obligation to purchase, or any other legal or equitable right affecting any land and buildings other than the Property.

14.3    Appurtenant Rights
    (a)    There is appurtenant to the Property each right and easement necessary for its proper and existing use, including without limitation, emergency escape routes. No right or easement is restricted in any way (including without limitation, a restriction on hours of use) or is capable of being lawfully interrupted or terminated by any person.

    (b)    The Company holds each right or easement appurtenant to:
        (i)    freehold Property, in fee simple; or
        (ii)    Property held by it under a lease, tenancy, or licence, for a term not less than the

            unexpired term of the lease, tenancy, or licence.

(c)     The principal means of access to the Property is sufficient for the existing use of the Property and are over roads which have been taken over by the local or other highway authority and which are maintainable at the public expense, and no means of access to the Property is shared with any other party nor subject to rights of determination by any other party.

(d)     Each service necessary for the Property's existing use (including without limitation, gas and water, sewerage, drainage, electricity, and telecommunications) is available to the Company.

**14.4**    **Outgoings**

The Property is not subject to any outgoings, other than property tax, water rates and insurance premiums and, in the case of leasehold, tenanted or licensed properties, rent, service charges and insurance premiums.

**14.5**    **Adverse Interests**

(a)     The Property is free from any Encumbrance securing the repayment of monies or any other obligation or liability of the Company or any other party.

(b)     Neither the Property nor any of its title deeds is subject to any agreement, obligation, condition, right, restrictive covenants, stipulations, easements, profits a prendre, wayleaves, licences, grants, restrictions, exception, reservation, overriding interests or other similar rights vested in third parties.

(c)     Where any of the matters referred to in paragraphs 14.4, 14.5(a) and 14.5(b) have been Disclosed in the Memorandum of Disclosure, the obligations and liabilities imposed and arising under them have been fully observed and performed, and any payments in respect of them due and payable have been fully paid on or before the relevant due date.

(d) The Property is free from any land charge, caveat, inhibition or notice, and no matter exists which is capable of registration against the Property.

(e) There is no person in possession or occupation of, or who has or claims a right or interest of any kind in, the Property adverse to the Company's interest.

14.6 Property Permits

(a) The Company has obtained each Property Permit [, details of which are set out in the Memorandum of Disclosure]. In particular:

(i) from the date of purchase of the Property by the Company, all requisite planning permission has been obtained for the development of the Property and since such date, no such permission has been suspended or called in and no application for planning permission is awaiting decision; and

(ii) from the date of purchase of the Property by the Company, building regulation consents have been obtained with respect to all development alterations and improvements to the Property since such date.

(b) The Company has complied and is complying in all respects with the terms and conditions of each Property Permit, orders and regulations issued under the relevant legislation relating to planning and use of real property and building regulation consents and bye-laws for the time being in force with respect to the Property and has performed and complied with each obligation, condition, restriction, agreement (including without limitation, the terms of any lease) and legal and administrative requirement affecting the Property, its ownership, occupation, possession or existing use and the Vendor is not aware of any breach thereof or of any intended or contemplated revocation of any such Property Permit.

(c) There is no outstanding and unobserved or unperformed obligation with respect to the Property necessary to comply with the requirements (whether formal or informal) of any competent authority exercising statutory or delegated powers.

(d) Each Property Permit is in force, unimpeachable and unconditional or subject only to a condition that has been satisfied. No expenditure or work is or will be necessary to comply with, maintain or obtain a Property Permit. To the best of the Vendor's knowledge, information and belief, no Property Permit will be revoked, suspended, cancelled, varied, or not renewed.

(e) Each action required for the renewal or extension of each Property Permit has been taken.

(f) No Property Permit will be revoked, suspended, cancelled, varied, or not renewed as a result of the execution or performance of this Agreement or any document to be executed at or before Completion.

14.7 Use and Construction

(a) The use of the Property is the permitted use for the purposes of any legislation relating to planning and use of real property and such permission is unconditional and not temporary or personal.

(b) The Property is not listed as being of special historic or architectural importance or located in a conservation area.

(c) Any permission necessary for the Property's existing use, its original construction and any subsequent alteration has been obtained and is in force, unimpeachable and unconditional or subject only to a condition that has been satisfied.

(d)    The Property is actively used by the Company in connection with the Business.

(e)    No demolition, development or construction work has been carried out in relation to the Property which would require any consent under the Developmental Control Laws or the relevant Government land grant without such consent having been properly obtained and any conditions or restrictions imposed upon the giving of such consent have been observed and performed.

(f)    No application by the Company under the Developmental Control Laws or relevant Government land grant in relation to demolition, development, or construction work or for change of use at the Property has been submitted or a decision in relation thereto appealed which application or appeal, as the case may be, is still pending and no application has been submitted and refused.

(g)    There are no circumstances or matters which would prevent any development, change of use, demolition, or construction work at the Property for which consent under the Development Control Laws, or the relevant Government land grant has been obtained.

14.8    Condition of the Property

(a)    There is no material deficiency which requires correction in the state or condition of any building or other structure on or forming part of the Property.

(b)    The buildings and other structures on the Property are in good and substantial repair and fit for the purposes for which they are used. No building or other structure on or forming part of the Property contains a deleterious substance or a substance which is not at the date of this Agreement used in generally accepted good buildings practice.

(c)    There are no disputes with any neighboring owner with respect to boundary walls and fences, or with respect to any easement or right over or means of access to the Property.

(d)    No flooding, subsidence, or other material defect of any kind (including without limitation, a design construction defect) affects or has affected the Property. The Property is not located in an area or subject to circumstances particularly susceptible to flooding.

(e)    [Where the Property comprises a building or other structure which was completed within five (5) years before the date of this Agreement, the Company obtained from each person involved in the design or construction of the building or other structure (including without limitation, a developer, landlord, contractor, sub-contractor, architect, engineer or surveyor) a warranty by the person, in the form that a prudent owner or occupier of the building or other structure would reasonably require, as to its design or construction or both, and each warranty is enforceable and may be assigned at least once.]

14.9    Adverse Orders

(a)    There are no compulsory notices, orders or resolutions affecting the Property which have been received by the Company, and there are no circumstances known to the Vendor which are likely to lead to any being made.

(b)    There are no closing, demolition or clearance orders, enforcement notices or stop notices affecting the Property which have been received by the Company, and there are no circumstances known to the Vendor which is likely to lead to any being made.

14.10    Insurance

(a)    The Property is insured in accordance with the terms

of the Policies disclosed to the Purchaser and none of which are subject to any special or unusual terms or restrictions or to the payment of any premium in excess of the normal rate for policies of the same kind.

(b) All premiums payable in respect of Policies with respect to the Property which have become due have been duly paid, and no circumstances have arisen which would vitiate or permit the insurers to avoid the Policies.

14.11 Property Proceedings:

There are, and during the two (2) years preceding the date of this Agreement have been, no outstanding actions, disputes, claims or demands between the Company and any third party relating to the Property or any neighboring property and no outstanding notice, judgement, order, decree, arbitral award or decision of a court, tribunal, arbitrator, or governmental agency affecting the Property.

14.12 Leasehold Properties:

Where the Company holds Property under a lease, tenancy, or licence:

(a) no person (including without limitation, the landlord or licensor) may bring the term to an end before the expiry of the lease, tenancy, or licence by effluxion of time (except by forfeiture);

(b) there is no fact or circumstance (and to the best of the Vendor's knowledge, information and belief, no fact or circumstance will within [six (6)] months from the date of this Agreement occur or arise) which (whether as a result of the acquisition of the Sale Shares by the Purchaser or otherwise):

(i) could entitle or require a person (including without limitation, a landlord or licensor) to forfeit or enter on, or take possession of, or occupy, the Property);

(ii)     could restrict or terminate the Company's continued and uninterrupted possession or occupation of the Property; or

(iii)     could prevent or restrict the Property's development for which planning permission has been or is expected to be obtained;

(c)     the Company has paid all rent and fees payable in respect of the Property and such rent and fees are not at the date of this Agreement being reviewed and cannot be reviewed [before Completion/for one (1) year after Completion];

(d)     no person (including without limitation, a landlord or licensor) has elected to waive, or indicated an intention to waive, an exemption from payment by the Company of goods and services tax in respect of a payment made under the lease, tenancy, or licence;

(e)     the Company has duly observed and performed the covenants on the part of the tenant and the conditions contained in any leases (which expression in this paragraph 14.12(e) includes underleases) or licences under which the Property is held and the last demand (or receipts for rent if issued) were unqualified, and all the leases and licences are valid and in full force;

(f)     all licences, consents and approvals required from the landlords and any superior landlords under any leases of the Property have been obtained, and the covenants on the part of the tenant contained in the licences, consents and approvals have been duly performed and observed;

(g)     no obligation necessary to comply with any notice or other requirement given by the landlord under any leases of the Property is outstanding or unobserved or unperformed;

(h)     there is no obligation to reinstate the Property by removing or dismantling any alteration made to it by the Company or any predecessor in title to the Company;

(i) the lease, tenancy or licence does not contain an unusually onerous covenant or condition, including without limitation, a covenant or condition allowing the landlord or licensor unreasonably to withhold or delay consent to an assignment of the whole Property or to an application to carry out a non-structural obligation;

(j) there is no material subsisting breach, nor any material non-observance of any covenant, condition or agreement contained in the lease, tenancy, or licence under which the Company holds its interest in the Property on the part of either the relevant landlord or licensor or the Company and no landlord or licensor has refused to accept rent or made any complaint or objection;

(k) there are no restrictions in the lease, tenancy or licence which prevent the Property being used now or in the future for the present use;

(l) no alterations has been made to the Property at the expense of the Company without all necessary consents and approvals and all such alterations to the Property are to be disregarded on rent reviews and do not have to be reinstated at the expiry of the term;

(m) the lease, tenancy or licence has been properly completed and stamped and are in the possession and under the control of the Company;

(n) where the Company is responsible for maintaining insurance of the Property, the Policy conforms in all respects with the requirements of the relevant lease, tenancy, or licence;

(o) Policies of insurance relating to the interior of the Property and their fixtures, fittings and contents have been affected by the Company, are current and valid, cover the full reinstatement value thereof and are not subject to any special or unusual terms or restrictions or to the payment of any premia in excess of the normal rate for policies of the same kind; and

(p)     There are no circumstances or matters which would affect the occupation or use of the Property by the Company or require the Company to surrender the Property.

14.13    Property subject to Occupational Interests
(a) Where the Property is subject to a lease, tenancy, or licence:

(i)     the lease, tenancy or licence is on tenant's or licensee's full repairing and insuring terms and contains no provisions which could materially or adversely affect the value of the Company's reversion;

(ii)    the tenant or licensee has in all material respects complied with its obligations under the lease, tenancy, or licence;

(iii)   the Company has not waived compliance with an obligation of the tenant or licensee, nor with an obligation of a surety for the tenant or licensee;

(iv)    no premium or rent has been taken, accepted, or agreed of an amount more than that legally permitted and no advance payment or computation of any future rent, fee or other payment under the lease, tenancy or licence has been accepted or agreed to be accepted;

(v)     the Company has taken no deposit of money or charge over a sum of money or fund from a tenant or licensee as security for compliance with any of its obligations; and

(vi)    The lease, tenancy or licence contains no

restriction on the election by the Company to waive an exemption from charging goods and services tax on a payment made by the tenant or licensee under the lease, tenancy, or licence.

(b) Save as set out in the Memorandum of Disclosure, the Company has not created, granted, or agreed to grant any lease, sub-lease, tenancy, sub-tenancy, licence, or other interest giving a person a right to use, possess or occupy the Property.

14.13 Outstanding Property Liabilities

(a) Except in relation to the Property, the Company has no liability arising out of a conveyance, transfer, lease, tenancy, licence, agreement, or other document relating to land, premises or an interest in land or premises.

(b) The Company has not given any guarantee or indemnity for any liability relating to the Property or any land and buildings.]

15. COMPUTERS AND COMPUTER SYSTEMS

15.1 IT System

(a) All IT System (including without limitation, computer servers) owned by the Company or used by or on behalf of the Company (including software, peripherals, communications links, and storage media):

(i) are in full operating order and are fulfilling the purposes for which they were acquired or are established in an efficient manner without material downtime or errors;

(ii) have adequate capacity for its present needs;

(iii) have adequate security, back-ups, duplication, hardware and software support and maintenance (including emergency cover) and trained personnel to ensure:

(A)    that breaches of security, errors and breakdowns are kept to a minimum; and

(B)    that no disruption will be caused to its business or any part thereof in the event of a breach of security, error, or breakdown;

(iv)    are properly documented by written technical descriptions and manuals so as to enable them to be used and operated by any reasonably qualified personnel; and

(v)    are under its sole control, are located in premises within Singapore owned or leased by it, are not shared with, or used by or on behalf of or accessible by any other person and (save for software licensed to it) are owned or leased by it.

(b)    All software used on or stored or resident in the said IT System:

(i)    perform efficiently in accordance with their respective specification and does not contain any defect or feature which may adversely affect their respective performance or the performance of any other software in the future or in any future circumstances;

(ii)    are lawfully held and used and does not infringe the copyright or other Intellectual Property Rights of any person and all copies held have been lawfully made;

(iii)    as to the copyright therein:

(A)    in the case of software written or commissioned by the Company, are owned exclusively by it, no other person has rights therein or rights to use copies of the software or source codes, and complete written listings and written copies of the source codes for the software are held by it;

(B)    in the case of standard package software purchased outright, are licensed to it on an express or implied licence which does not require it to make any further payments, are not terminable without its consent and which imposes no restrictions (save as to copying) on the use or transfer of the software; and

(C)    in the case of all other software, is licensed to it on the terms of a written licence (a true and complete copy of which is annexed to the Memorandum of Disclosure) which requires payment by it of a fixed annual licence fee at a rate not exceeding that paid in the financial year ended the Balance Sheet Date but (save for reasonable fees for software support) requires it to make no further or other payment, is not terminable (save for failure to pay the licence fee) without its consent and imposes no restrictions (save as to copying) on the use or transfer of the software;

(iv)    do not contain any software virus and have not within the last [three (3)] years been infected by any software virus or accessed by any unauthorised person.

(c)    No software owned by or licensed to the Company is

used by or licensed or sub-licensed by it to any other person.

(d) All records and data stored by electronic means are capable of ready access through the present computer systems of the Company.

(e) No person is in a position, by virtue of his rights in, knowledge of or access to any of the IT System used by the Company or any part of them (including software) to demand any payment in excess of any current licence fee or in excess of reasonable remuneration for services rendered, or to impose any onerous condition, in order to preserve the proper and efficient functioning of the computer systems in the future.

(f) The appropriate employees are adequately trained to enable them to use and operate the IT System owned or used by the Company (including software, peripherals, and storage media) to the full extent of the capabilities of those systems without assistance from any other person. The IT System includes sufficient user information to enable reasonably skilled personnel in the field to use and operate the IT System without the need for further assistance.

(g) In relation to the IT System (including without limitation, computer servers) owned by the Company or used by or on behalf of the Company (including software, peripherals, communications links, and storage media):

(i) such IT System will continue to process data correctly and consistently with reference to any and all dates, including without limitation, any date in any century or leap year;

(ii) the performance and functionality of such IT System will not be adversely affected by any date, or any change of date used by or stored within such IT System, including without limitation, any date or change of date after the Completion Date; and

(iii) all output from such IT System, including without limitation, any output for any interface to other hardware, software or systems will in relation to any date contained within such output explicitly and unambiguously identify the date in full, including without limitation, the century within which the date falls.

(h) Save to the extent provided in the IT Contracts, the Company is the legal and beneficial owners of the IT System free from Encumbrances. The Company has obtained all necessary rights from third parties to enable them to make exclusive and unrestricted use of the IT System.

15.2 IT Contracts

(a) The IT Contracts are valid, and binding and no act or omission has occurred which would (if necessary, with the giving of notice or lapse of time) constitute a breach of any such contract.

(b) There are and have been no claims, disputes or proceedings arising under any IT Contracts.

(c) None of the IT Contracts are liable to be terminated or would otherwise be materially affected by the sale of the Sale Shares, and to the best of the Vendor's knowledge, information and belief, the IT Contracts will be renewed on the same or substantially the same terms when they expire.

15.3 General

The Company has in place a disaster recovery plan which is fully documented and would enable the business of the Company to continue if there were significant damage to or destruction of some or all of the IT System. A copy of the plan is attached to the Memorandum of Disclosure.

Complete and accurate particulars of the IT System and all IT Contracts are set out in the Memorandum of Disclosure.

## 16. ENVIRONMENTAL MATTERS

16.1    Compliance with Environmental Law:
The Company has at all times complied with all Environmental Law in force, relevant or applicable to the Company in Singapore or elsewhere and there is nothing in, on, over or under the Property the presence, existence or condition of which constitutes a breach of such Environmental Law nor is there or has there been any manufacturing, storage, generation, servicing, treatment, disposal or other process carried on at the Property in such a way as to amount to a breach of the same.

16.2    Hazardous Substance:
No toxic industrial waste or toxic substance (as defined in any Environmental Law) or any other Hazardous Substance (howsoever termed), including without limitation, polychlorinated biphenyls, radioactive material, lead, asbestos-containing material, incinerator, landfill, septic, wastewater treatment or other disposal system or underground or above-ground storage tank (active or inactive) is or has been present at, on or under, or has been spilt, leaked, released, deposited, discharged or disposed in the soil or water in, under, around or upon the Property or any property previously owned, leased or operated by the Company.

16.3    Environmental Proceedings
No notice, notification, demand, request for information, citation, summons, order or complaint has been received from any third party (including any employee of the Company or governmental, regulatory, supervisory or administrative body), no penalty has been assessed and no action, suit or proceeding is pending, or to the knowledge of the Vendor,

threatened (nor to the knowledge of the Vendor is there any investigation or review pending) by any governmental authority or other person with respect to any matters relating to the Company arising out of any Environmental Law.

16.4    Environmental Investigation
No property or other asset now or previously owned, leased or operated by the Company is listed or, to the knowledge of the Vendor, proposed for listing on the list of sites requiring investigation or clean-up. There has been no environmental investigation, study, audit, test, review, or other analysis conducted of which the Vendor is aware in relation to tmhe current or prior business of the Company or any property or facility now or previously owned, leased or operated by the Company which has not been made available to the Purchaser at least [10] Business Days prior to the date of this Agreement.

16.5    Environmental Liabilities:
There are no liabilities of or relating to the business of the Company of any kind whatsoever, whether accrued, contingent, absolute, determined, determinable or otherwise, arising under or relating to any Environmental Law (including any liability to make good, repair, re-instate or clean up land or another asset owned, occupied, possessed or used by the Company on or before the date of this Agreement) and there are no facts, conditions, situations or set of circumstances which could reasonably be expected to result in or be the basis for any such liability.

17.  TERMS OF TRADE AND BUSINESS
17.1    Customers and Suppliers
(a)    During the year prior to the date of this Agreement, no substantial supplier or customer has:
(i)    stopped, or indicated an intention to stop, trading with the Company;
(ii)    reduced, or indicated an intention to

      reduce, substantially its trading with the Company;

(iii) changed, or indicated an intention to change, substantially the terms on which it is prepared to trade with the Company,

and to the best of the information, knowledge and belief of the Vendor, no substantial supplier or customer is likely to do so within [12] months after Completion.

(b) The loss of any single supplier to or customer of the Company would not have an effect on its business.

(c) So far as the Vendor is aware, there has been no express communication by any customer, supplier and/or employee of the Company which would indicate that the attitudes, actions or prices of such customer, supplier and/or employee (with regard to the Company) will be prejudicially affected by the execution or completion of this Agreement or any document to be executed in connection with this Agreement. The expression "so far as the Vendor is aware" shall be deemed to refer to the knowledge of the Vendor after having made all reasonable endeavors to ensure that all information given, referred to or reflected in this statement is accurate in all material aspects.

(d) The change in the shareholdings of the Company upon Completion will not result in the termination of or materially affect any agreement or arrangement between the Company and its suppliers or customers.

17.2 Product Liabilities:

(a) Save for any condition or warranty implied by law, the Company has not given any guarantee, condition or warranty or made any representation in respect of goods or services supplied or contracted to be supplied by it or accepted any obligation which could give rise to any liability after any such goods or services have been supplied by it.

(b) The Company has no reason to believe that any products or line of goods currently in stock or in the course of production or any material proportion thereof is not or will not prove to be of merchantable quality and fit for its purpose.

(c) The Company has not received notice of any claim which remains outstanding alleging any defect in or lack of fitness for the purpose of any goods supplied by the Company, nor are there any circumstances which could give rise to any such claim.

(d) The Company has not received notice of any claim which remains outstanding alleging the failure to perform, either properly or at all, any services performed or to be performed by the Company nor are there any circumstances which could give rise to any such claims.

(e) The Company has not agreed to take back any defective goods or to effect repairs to any goods free of charge or otherwise or to issue a credit note or to write off or reduce indebtedness in respect of any goods or services supplied by it.

17.3 Computer Records:
None of the records, systems, data, or information of the Company is recorded, stored, maintained, operated or otherwise wholly or partly dependent on or held or accessible by any means (including without limitation, an electronic, mechanical, or photographic process computerized or not) which are not under the exclusive ownership and direct control of the Company.

18. CORPORATE MATTERS

18.1 Due Incorporation:
The Company has been duly incorporated and is validly existing under the laws of its country of incorporation and is

not in receivership or liquidation.

18.2    Share Capital

(a)    The Company has not exercised any lien over any of its issued shares.

(b)    The Company has not reduced, repaid, or purchased any of its share capital, and there are no options or other agreements outstanding which call for the issue of or accord to any person the right to call for the issue of any shares in the capital of the Company or the right to require the creation of any Encumbrance over any shares in its share capital.

(c)    Except for this Agreement, there is no option, right to acquire, mortgage, charge, pledge, lien or other form of security or Encumbrance on, over or affecting the shares or capital in, or any of the assets or businesses of, the Company and there is no agreement or commitment to give or create any of the foregoing.

18.3    Compliance

(a)    The Company has complied with its memorandum and articles of association (or the equivalent constitutive documents) in all respects and none of the activities, agreements, commitments, or rights of the Company is ultra vires or unauthorised.

(b)    All governmental approvals, licences and authorizations which were necessary or desirable in connection with the incorporation of the Company, the allotment or transfer of shares in the Company to the present and former holders thereof and the activation of the Company (including the appointment of directors) were duly obtained and such approvals, licences, and authorizations (and all amendments and supplements thereto) have been Disclosed to the Purchaser in the Memorandum of Disclosure.

19. SUBSIDIARIES AND ASSOCIATED COMPANIES

The Company is not the legal or beneficial owner or holder of any share or has any interest of any description in any other corporation and does not have any associated company (that is to say, a company which falls to be treated as such for the purposes of the FRS).

20. STATUTORY AND OTHER REQUIREMENTS, CONSENTS AND LICENCES

(a)  The Company has carried on its business in accordance with applicable laws, regulations, and by-laws in its country of incorporation or elsewhere and so far as the Vendor is aware in any relevant country and there is no investigation or enquiry by, or order, decree, or judgment of, any court or any governmental agency or regulatory body outstanding or anticipated against the Company or which may have an adverse effect upon its assets or business. The expression "so far as the Vendor is aware" shall be deemed to refer to the knowledge of the Vendor after having used all reasonable endeavors to ensure that the information given, referred to or reflected in this statement is accurate in all material aspects.

(b)  All statutory and other requirements applicable to the carrying on of the business of the Company as now carried on, and all conditions applicable to any licences and consents involved in the carrying on of such business, have been complied with and the Vendor is not aware of any breach thereof or of any intended or contemplated refusal or revocation of any such licence or consent.

(c)  The Company has obtained and has complied with the terms and conditions of each Permit, details of which are disclosed in the Memorandum of Disclosure.

(d)  Each Permit is in force, unimpeachable and unconditional or subject only to a condition that has been satisfied. No expenditure or work is or will be necessary to comply with, maintain or obtain a Permit. To the best of the Vendor's knowledge, information and belief, no Permit will be revoked, suspended, cancelled, varied, or not renewed.

(e) Each action required for the renewal or extension of each Permit has been taken.

(f) No Permit will be revoked, suspended, cancelled, varied, or not renewed as a result of the execution or performance of this Agreement or any document to be executed at or before Completion.

21. FEES, COMMISSIONS AND BROKERAGE

(a) No person is entitled to recover from the Company any finders' fees, brokerage, or other commission in connection with the sale and purchase of the Sale Shares under this Agreement.

(b) No claim or demand for payment of commission, legal or accountancy fees or other payments has been or will be made against the Company by any person directly or indirectly in connection with the negotiations leading to this Agreement.

22. COMPETITION

The Company is not a party to, or is engaged in, any agreement, arrangement, practice or conduct which would contravene any provision of the Competition Act (list relevant country law).

23. LITIGATION

23.1 Litigation

(a) Neither the Company nor a person for whose acts or defaults the Company may be vicariously liable is involved or has during the [two (2)] years prior to the date of this Agreement been involved, in a civil, criminal, arbitration, administrative or other proceeding (other than as plaintiff in the collection of debts arising in the ordinary course of its business).

(b) To the best of the information, knowledge and belief of the Vendor, no fact or circumstance exists which might give rise to a civil, criminal, arbitration, administrative or other proceeding involving the Company or a person for whose acts or defaults the Company may be vicariously liable (other than involvement as plaintiff in the collection of debts arising in the ordinary course of its business).

(c)     Neither the Company nor any person for whose acts or defaults the Company may be vicariously liable has committed any criminal, illegal or other unlawful act or any breach of contract or statutory duty or any tortious or other act or default which could lead to a claim or proceedings against the Company or give rise to or increase the liability or obligation of the Company or which could entitle any other person to terminate any contract to which the Company is a party.

23.2     Judgments

(a)     There is not in force any court injunction, order or directive restraining or restricting the Company from carrying on its business or any part thereof or entering into this Agreement.

(b)     There is no outstanding judgment, order or decree of any court, tribunal or regulatory or government body or any undertaking to any court, judicial authority or regulatory or government body or any outstanding arbitration award against the Company or a person for whose acts or defaults the Company may be vicariously liable.

(c)     There are no civil, criminal, administrative or disciplinary or arbitration proceedings in progress, pending or threatened against the Company or a person for whose acts or defaults the Company may be vicariously liable and there are no facts likely to give rise to any such proceedings.

23.3     Investigations

There is not and has not been any governmental or other investigations, inquiries, or disciplinary proceedings by or before any regulatory, administrative, supervisory or government body concerning the Company, whether on-going, pending or threatened and to the best of the information, knowledge and belief of the Vendor, no fact or circumstance exist which might give rise to any such investigation, inquiry, or proceedings.

23.4 Unlawful Payments

Neither the Company nor any person for whose acts or defaults the Company may be vicariously liable has induced a person to enter into an agreement or arrangement with the Company by means of an unlawful or immoral payment, bribe, contribution, gift, or other inducement or has given or offered or made an unlawful or immoral payment, bribe, contribution, gift, or other inducement to a government official or employee.

23.5 Convictions

The Company has not been convicted of any offence. No officer, employee, agent or former officer, agent or employee of the Company has been convicted of any offences in relation to the Company, and no employee has, so far as the Vendor is aware, been convicted of any offence (save for any traffic offence) which reflects upon his suitability to hold his position or upon the reputation of the Company. The expression "so far as the Vendor is aware" shall be deemed to refer to the knowledge of the Vendor after having made all reasonable endeavors to ensure that all information given, referred to or reflected in this statement is accurate in all material aspects.

24. INSOLVENCY

24.1 Winding up and Administration

No order has been made or petition presented or resolution passed for the winding-up or administration or for the appointment of a provisional liquidator of the Company, nor are there any grounds on which any person would be entitled to have the Company wound-up or placed in administration, nor has any person threatened to present such a petition or convened or threatened to convene a meeting of the Company to consider a resolution to wind up the Company or any other resolutions, nor has any step been taken in relation to the Company under the law relating to insolvency or the relief of debtors in any part of the world.

24.2    Receivership
No person has appointed or threatened to appoint or become entitled to appoint a receiver or receiver and manager or other similar officer of the Company's business or assets or any part of them.

24.3    Arrangements
No composition in satisfaction of the debts of the Company, or scheme of arrangement of its affairs, or compromise or arrangement between it and its creditors and/or members or any class of its creditors and/or members, has been proposed, sanctioned, or approved.

24.4    Payment of Debts
The Company has not ceased trading nor stopped payment to its creditors and there are no grounds on which the Company could be found to be unable to pay its debts within the meaning of Section 254 of the Companies Act.

24.5    Distress
No distress, execution or other process has been levied on any asset owned or used by the Company, nor has any person threatened any such distress, execution, or other process.

24.6    Unsatisfied Judgments
There is no unsatisfied judgment or court order outstanding against the Company.

24.7    Events of Default
    (a)    No event has occurred causing or which upon intervention or notice by any third party may cause any floating charge created by the Company to crystallize or any charge created by the Company to become enforceable, nor has any such crystallization occurred nor is such enforcement in process.

    (b)    In relation to any property or assets held by the Company under any hire purchase, conditional sale, chattel leasing or retention of title agreement or otherwise belonging to a third party, no event has occurred which entitles, or which upon intervention or notice by a third party may entitle, the third party to repossess the property or assets concerned or terminate the agreement or any licence in respect of the same.

24.8    Undervalue/preference
The Company has not at any time during the two (2) years immediately prior to the date of this Agreement:
    (i)    entered into a transaction with any person at an undervalue (as referred to in section 98 of the Bankruptcy Act (list relevant country law)); or
    (ii)    been given a preference by any person (as referred to in section 99 of the Bankruptcy Act (list relevant country law)).

25. EFFECT OF SALE OF SALE SHARES
Neither the acquisition of the Sale Shares by the Purchaser nor compliance with the terms of this Agreement will:
    (i)    cause the Company to lose the benefit of any right or privilege it presently enjoys;
    (ii)    relieve any person of any obligation to the Company (whether contractual or otherwise) or enable any person to determine any such obligation or any right or benefit enjoyed by the Company, or to exercise any right in respect of the

Company; or

(iii) give rise to, or cause to become exercisable, any right of pre-emption over the Sale Shares.

## Comments

### Representations

Representations are statements of fact made by one party to another, usually before or at the time a contract is formed. These statements are designed to induce the other party into entering into the contract. For example, a seller might represent that they are the legal owner of a property they are selling.

If a representation turns out to be false, it may give rise to a right to terminate the contract or to claim damages, often under the doctrine of "fraudulent misrepresentation" or "innocent misrepresentation," depending on jurisdiction and circumstances.

### Warranties

Warranties are assurances or guarantees that a particular fact or condition is true or will occur. Unlike representations, warranties typically extend for a specific period and relate to the performance of the contract. For example, a manufacturer may provide a warranty that a product will be free from defects for one year.

If a warranty is breached, the aggrieved party usually has a right to remedies such as repair, replacement, or monetary damages, depending on the terms of the contract and applicable law.

### Remedies:

The remedies for breach of representation can include contract termination and damages, potentially even if the breach was unintentional. Remedies for breach of warranty are generally limited to what is specified in the contract (e.g., repair, replacement, or damages).

In order not to clutter up the main agreement, this "Representations and Warranties" clause should be added as Schedule and relevant reference made in the Interpretation / Construction clause.

### 53. Reserved Matters

List of Reserved Matters

So long as ABC and XYZ (and/or their respective Affiliates) respectively hold not less than __ percent of the issued, subscribed, and paid-up share capital of the JV, the Parties agree that no action shall be taken by the JV in respect of the matters listed hereinbelow, without prior written consent of the Parties:

1. Any amendment to the Certificate of Incorporation, the Memorandum of Association, or the Articles of Association.

2. Any increase or reduction in the authorized, issued, subscribed and paid-up share capital.

3. Any issuance and/or allotment of any securities or instruments including equity or preference shares or debentures.

4. Any recommendation or declaration regarding dividends (whether interim or final) and any other distribution of profits or assets to the shareholders of JV.

5. Any resolution for long-term borrowings or financial assistance.

6. Any resolution for borrowing working capital finances over and above that which is required in the usual course of business or approved in the [annual business plan].

7. Any sale, amalgamation, reconstruction, or liquidation of the JV or lifting out or disposition in any other matter of the whole or substantial part of the capital assets of the JV.

8. Any activity or transaction outside the ordinary scope of the business of the JV.

9. The purchase by the JV of shares, stocks, or debentures of any body-corporate.

10. The disposal by the JV of any assets or undertaking with an aggregate value of [ten percent (10%)] or more of the net worth of the JV (calculated at the time of the proposed disposal) in any one (1) financial year of the JV.

11. Acquiring from, or granting to, third parties by licence or otherwise trademarks, technology, patents, or intellectual

property rights, provided that nothing herein shall limit or affect the JV's power to sub-contract any part of manufacture of the Kiosks and authorize the sub-contractors to use the trademarks, technology, patents, or intellectual property rights.

12. Making any material alteration or deviation in the business of the JV.

13. The making of political or charitable contributions which have an annual aggregate value or are likely to involve annual expenditure by the JV or any subsidiary of the JV in excess of USD10,000/- or the equivalent in USD or such other amount as parties holding shares representing not less than [forty-nine (49%)] of the issued share capital of the JV may from time to time agree.

14. The employment, discharge, conditions of service, scope of authority, powers to operate and delegate and any variation of any of the foregoing (including those in the agreement between the Managing Director and the JV), of the Managing Director.

15. Subject to Article ___ above (Appointment of Directors), appointment of any director in any increase or reduction in the number of directors.

16. The Appointment and removal and the terms of reference and service/employment contracts of each of the CEO, Chairman, General Manager, Chief Financial Officer, and Secretary of the JV.

17. Any change in the Auditor(s) of the JV.

18. Approval of the Accounts and Reports to be presented before the members in the General Meeting(s).

19. Undertaking any new business or substantial expansion of contemplated business or discontinuation of manufacture of any or all of the Kiosks.

20. Subject to Articles ___ and ___ above (Transfer of Shares), approval or refusal of transfer of shares.

21. Except as provided in this MoU, appointment of any sole selling agent/sole distributor for the sale of any Kiosks manufactured by the JV.

22. Initiation of, or an agreement to settle, any dispute, litigation, arbitration, or other proceeding with any third party, whether as petitioner/plaintiff or respondent/defendant, in respect of matters having a substantial bearing on the JV's activities or exceeding in value of [USD] one hundred million (USD100,000,000/-) or such other higher figure as the Parties may agree from time to time.

23. Any pledge, mortgage, hypothecation, or encumbrance by the JV of any of its assets other than in the normal course of business.

24. The accrual(s) by the JV of any liability or guarantee for any obligation of third party(ies) other than in the normal course of business.

25. The establishment of and any material variations of the JV's financial policy including (without limitation of the foregoing) the following aspects, in particular:

    a. The nature and structure of the JV's share capital;
    b. The determination of maximum total debt expressed as a percentage of equity;
    c. The determination of desirable interest cover rates;
    d. The composition and duration of long-term interest-bearing debt;
    e. The undertaking of offshore finance and any uncovered foreign currency commitments;
    f. The accounting policies as reflected in the annual financial statements of the JV from time to time.

26. The remuneration payable to a director for services rendered in his capacity as a director of the JV.

27. Approval of [annual business plan] and/or modifications.

28. Entry into any partnership or joint venture by the JV or any subsidiary of the JV.

29. Any proposal for the winding up of the JV or any filing by the JV for liquidation, receivership or reorganization under any insolvency laws or any similar action, except in the case where the JV is proposed to be wound up or liquidated.

## Comments

A set of decisions or actions that cannot be undertaken without the specific approval of a particular party or parties to the contract. Essentially, reserved matters are items that are considered so significant that they require special attention and cannot be handled through ordinary business processes or governance.

## 54. Restrictions of Share Transfer

1. During the term of this Agreement, a Shareholder shall not Transfer, assign, pledge, give, create any interest or Encumbrance over or dispose of, any Equity Shares (or instruments or securities convertible into or exchangeable with Equity Shares or which confer a right to subscribe to Equity Shares at a later date) held by it in the Company without the prior written consent of the remaining Shareholders. The restriction contained in the preceding sentence shall not, however, apply:
   a. after the completion of the IPO of the Company on the [Party A] Stock Exchange, at a valuation of the Company which shall be acceptable to the Shareholders; or
   b. in case of sale of the entire share capital of the Company to a third party buyer; or, (iii) with respect to any charges created in favor of banks or financial institutions in connection with raising genuine project financing for any of the Projects promoted, managed or undertaken by the Company.
2. Without prejudice to the generality of the foregoing Clause [Party A], at no point of time shall any Party Transfer any of the Equity Shares (or instruments or securities convertible into or exchangeable with Equity Shares or which confer a right to subscribe to Equity Shares at a later date) held by them to any Person without first giving effect to the rights of the other Parties provided for in Clauses [x] [Right Of First Refusal] and Clause [x] [Tag Along Right).

**Comments**

Other Types of Restrictions on Share Transfer:

1. ***Right of First Refusal***: This allows existing shareholders the

option to buy shares before the owner sells them to an external third party.

2.  **Drag-Along Rights**: These allow majority shareholders to force minority shareholders to join in the sale of the company.

3.  **Tag-Along Rights**: These allow minority shareholders to join a sale initiated by majority shareholders.

4.  **Pre-emptive Rights**: Similar to the Right of First Refusal but gives existing shareholders the right to purchase additional shares before the company offers them to external parties.

5.  **Lock-In Period**: Specifies a set amount of time during which shares cannot be sold.

6.  **Approval Clause**: Requires that the transfer of shares be approved by a specific majority of shareholders or a board of directors.

Effects on the Contract and Parties:

1.  **Liquidity**: These restrictions can make it more challenging to sell shares, affecting the liquidity of an investment in the company.

2.  **Control**: By governing who can and cannot own shares, these clauses can help existing shareholders maintain control over the company.

3.  **Valuation**: Certain restrictions may potentially lower the market value of shares since they limit the ease with which they can be sold.

4.  **Long-term Alignment**: They may ensure that shareholders are committed to the company for the long term, discouraging quick sales that could disrupt the business.

5.  **Due Diligence**: For potential new shareholders, the transfer restrictions require a heightened level of due diligence to understand the limitations on their investment.

6.  **Complexity**: The more complicated the restrictions, the more difficult it may be to attract new investors or to sell the company.

7.  **Legal Risk**: Failure to comply with these restrictions can result in legal consequences, including the possibility of reversing

the transaction.

8.    ***Negotiation and Exit Strategy***: Knowing these restrictions is crucial during any negotiation for investment or the sale of the company, as they can influence the bargaining power of each party.

## 55. Right of First Refusal

1.    Prior to the completion of an IPO, the Existing Shareholders shall have the right to be offered the shares which the other Party proposes to sell to any independent third party(ies). It is however clarified that on receiving any offer from any independent third party and at least [5] Business Days prior to entering into any contractual commitment with such third party offer, the Existing Shareholder, as the case may be, shall inform the other Party and the Board of receipt of such offer, and provide all relevant details (like number of shares offered to be purchased by such third party, the price per share offered by the third party, etc.).

2.    None of the Existing Shareholders may sell any of their Equity Shares to a third party without first offering the said Equity Shares ("Offered Shares") to the other Party. Such other Party shall have a right, but not the obligation, to purchase its pro rata share of the Offered Shares from such selling Prior Shareholder or Investor.

3.    Within five (5) Business Days of agreeing to sell all or any of the Equity Shares or at least thirty (30) days before the date of the proposed sale (whichever is earlier), each Existing Shareholder, as the case may be ("Selling Shareholder"), shall send a written notice (the "Sale Notice") to the Existing Shareholder, as the case may be ("Right Holder"), setting forth in detail the terms of the proposed sale, including the name of the person/s to whom the sale is proposed to be made ("Purchaser"), the proposed sale price per Share ("Third Party Price"), the date of the proposed sale (which shall not be less than thirty (30) days from the date of receipt of the Sale Notice) and the number of Equity Shares proposed to be sold ("Sale Shares").

4. Upon receipt of the Sale Notice, the Right Holder shall have the right, exercisable at its sole discretion to purchase the Sale Shares at the Third-Party Price by serving upon the Selling Shareholder a written notice in that regard within 15 Business Days of receipt of the Sale Notice by the Right Holder on the terms and conditions mentioned in the Sale Notice ("Right of First Refusal").

5. The Parties agree that the Right Holder may, at its sole discretion, choose not to exercise the Right of First Refusal. In the event that the Right Holder does not wish to exercise the Right of First Refusal, it shall inform the Selling Shareholder of the same within 15 Business Days of receipt of the Sale Notice.

6. If the Right Holder exercises its Right of First Refusal as mentioned above, within 60 Business Days, subject to the necessary regulatory consents, the Selling Shareholder shall tender the Sale Shares to the Right Holder and on the same Business Day the Right Holder shall pay the Selling Shareholder the consideration for the Sale Shares at the Third-Party Price.

7. If the Right Holder does not exercise the Right of First Refusal and does not serve a written notice upon the Selling Shareholder within the time period specified in Clause 3 above, then the Selling Shareholder may sell the Sale Shares to the Purchaser at the Third Party Price as mentioned in the Sale Notice, provided no such sale shall be made by any Existing Shareholder to a Competitor of the Company, without the prior written consent of the Existing Shareholder.

8. Provided that upon the transfer of the Shares under this Clause, the transferee shall be bound to execute a Deed of Adherence in the form attached as Schedule _ hereto if the transferee is not already a party to this Agreement and shall become a party to this Agreement in the same capacity as the transferring Shareholder and such other documents as may be required for this purpose.

9. Notwithstanding anything contained in Clause 1 and 2 of this Clause [x] [Right of First Refusal], such Right of First Refusal

shall not be available in favor of the investor where such sale or transfer is amongst the Existing Shareholders inter-se and/or where such sale or transfer is to an Affiliate.

10. It is further clarified that the provisions of this Clause [x] [Right of First Refusal] shall cease to have effect upon the completion of an IPO.

## Comments

A Right of First Refusal (ROFR) is a provision that gives one party the option to enter into a business transaction with the other party before the latter can negotiate with third parties. Essentially, if one party decides they want to sell an asset that is subject to a ROFR clause, they must first offer it to the other party under the same terms and conditions as they would to a third party. Only if the other party declines can the asset be sold to someone else.

### 56. Right of Set-Off

No Party can clear its own debts arising from this Agreement with the debts of the other Party arising from any other agreement entered or to be entered to by the Parties.

## Comments

The right of setoff (sometimes spelled "set-off" or "offset") allows a party to a contract to deduct a debt that is owed to them by the other party from a debt that they owe to that other party. Essentially, the amounts owed are "set off" against each other, often reducing or eliminating the obligation to pay the full amount of one of the debts.

### 57. Rights & Remedies

The rights and remedies reserved in this Agreement by a Party upon breach by the other Party are cumulative and in addition to all other rights and remedies provided in equity or at law. Waiver by either party of any breach of, or failure to comply with the other Party with a provision of this Agreement shall not be construed as or constitute a continuing waiver of such provision or a waiver of any other breach or failure to comply with any other provision of this Agreement.

## 58. Rights of Third Parties and Fiduciary Relationships

Save as expressly referred to herein, a person who is not a party to this Agreement shall have no rights under the [Singapore] Contracts (Right of Third Parties) Act, Chapter 53B to enforce or enjoy any of its terms. Notwithstanding any provision to the contrary herein, no consent of any third party is required for any variation (including any release or compromise of any liability under) or termination of this Agreement.

**Comments**
A "third party" refers to an individual or entity that is not a party to the contract but may be affected by it or have certain rights or obligations under it. Generally, a contract binds only the parties that have entered into the agreement, and third parties have no obligations or benefits under that contract.

Some exceptions are:
- Third-party beneficiary
- Assignment and delegation
- Tort liability
- Agency relationships

The Contracts (Rights of Third Parties) Act (Cap. 53B of Singapore) shall not under any circumstances apply to this Agreement and any Person who is not a party to this Agreement (whether or not such person shall be named, referred to, or otherwise identified, or shall form part of a class of persons so named, referred to, or identified, in this Agreement) shall have no right whatsoever under the Contracts (Rights of Third Parties) Act (Cap. 53B of Singapore) to enforce this Agreement or any of its terms.

Nothing contained in this Agreement shall be deemed or construed by the Parties or by any third party to create any rights, obligations, or interests in third parties, or to create the relationship of principal and agent, partnership, or joint venture between the Parties

### 59. Rules of Construction

**Comments**

See "Construction" and "Interpretation" in these Common Contract Clauses.

### 60. Severability / Invalidity

Each provision of this Agreement shall, to the extent possible, be interpreted in such manner to be effective and valid under applicable law, but if any provision of this Agreement shall be invalid or rendered invalid or prohibited under such applicable law, such invalidity shall not affect the validity or conflict of the other provisions of this Agreement.

[or]

Each provision of this Agreement shall, to the extent possible, be interpreted in such manner as to be effective and valid under applicable law, but, if any provision of this Agreement shall be invalid or prohibited under such applicable law, such invalidity shall not affect the validity of the other provisions of this Agreement. The said other provisions shall continue in full force and effect unless such unenforceable provision shall materially affect the essence of the Agreement and the Party benefiting from the said unenforceable provision does not waive its rights to benefit therefrom.

**Comments**

Severability refers to a provision that allows a court to remove or "sever" invalid, illegal, or unenforceable terms from a contract without affecting the validity and enforceability of the remaining provisions. In other words, if a certain provision of a contract is found to be unenforceable or illegal, the severability clause ensures that the rest of the contract can still be legally binding on the parties involved.

### 61. Survival

Any provision of this Agreement which can reasonably be construed to survive the expiration or termination of this Agreement, including the indemnification and confidentiality provisions set forth herein, shall survive such expiration or termination of this Agreement, till three years.

**Comments**

This clause generally stipulates that certain provisions will continue to apply even after the contract has terminated or expired. Survival clauses are included in contracts to outline which obligations will "survive" the end of the contract term. These clauses are particularly useful when the nature of the agreement necessitates ongoing obligations, such as confidentiality, indemnification, or the settling of final accounts.

A survival clause will specify which provisions survive and for how long they will continue to be effective. For example, a confidentiality clause might survive the termination of the contract for a specified number of years to protect sensitive information that was shared during the course of the contractual relationship.

Generally, the matters that may come under the Survival clause are:
- Definitions and Interpretation
- Non-competition and non-solicitation
- Accrued Rights
- Termination
- Notices
- Third Party Rights
- Dispute Resolution
- Inventions & Intellectual Property Rights
- Indemnification
- Confidential Information
- Warranties
- Conflicts of Interest
- Publicity
- Remedies
- Insurance
- Compliance with Laws
- Personal Data Protection

Miscellaneous (usually the boilerplate clauses).

The comments to this "survival" clause are particularly useful when some over-zealous lawyer puts in clauses and their numbers without mentioning which section or clause they are really supposed to belong to.

## 62. Tag-along Rights

1. Without prejudice to the Investor's Right of First Offer, if the Prior Shareholders propose to Transfer any or all of their shareholding in the Company and the Investor permits such Transfer the Prior Shareholders shall each provide the Investor a Tag Along Right in respect of their pro rata shareholding on a Fully Diluted Basis. Furthermore, it shall be the responsibility of the Prior Shareholders to ensure the rights of the Investor under this Clause are given effect.

2. If the Prior Shareholders propose to Transfer any or all of their shareholding in the Company, which is likely to result in a Change in Control, the Investor shall have the right to Transfer its entire shareholding in the Company to the Buyer (as defined hereafter) on the terms and conditions as set out in this Clause ("Tag Along Right").

3. Notwithstanding anything contained in Clause 1 and 2 above, such Tag Along Right shall not be available in favor of the Investor where Transfer is amongst the Prior Shareholders inter-se and/or where such Transfer is to an Affiliate of the Prior Shareholders.

4. Within five [(5)] Business Days of agreeing to sell all or any of Shares held by the Prior Shareholders or at least thirty [(30)] days before the date of the proposed sale (whichever is earlier), the Prior Shareholders, shall send written notice (the "Offer Notice") to the Investor, setting forth in detail the terms of the proposed sale, including the name of the person(s) to whom the sale is proposed to be made ("Buyer"), the proposed sale price ("Sale Price"), the date of the proposed sale (which shall not be less than thirty [30] days from the date of receipt of the Offer Notice by the Investor)

and the number of shares proposed to be sold by the Prior Shareholders ("Sale Shares").

5.      Upon receipt of the Offer Notice, the Investor shall have the option, exercisable at its sole discretion to sell its pro rata shareholding on a Fully Diluted Basis, in the total issued and paid up share capital of the Company, to the Buyer, at the Sale Price by serving upon the Prior Shareholders, a written notice in that regard within thirty [30] days of receipt of the Offer Notice by the Investor, individually on the terms and conditions mentioned in the Offer Notice ("Tag Along Option").

6.      If the Investor exercises its Tag Along Option as mentioned above, then the Prior Shareholders, shall ensure that the Buyer purchases the number of the Investor Shares mentioned in the notice by the Investor along with the Sale Shares mentioned in the Offer Notice at the Sale Price and on the terms mentioned in the Offer Notice. The Prior Shareholders shall ensure that the Buyer completes the purchase of the Investor Shares at the same time as completion of purchase of the Sale Shares held by the Prior Shareholders.

7.      If the Investor does not exercise its Tag Along Option and does not serve a written notice upon the Prior Shareholders within the time period specified in Clause 6 above, then the Prior Shareholders, may sell the Sale Shares (not exceeding the number mentioned in the Offer Notice) to the Buyer at the Sale Price and on the terms mentioned in the Offer Notice (and not at any other price or on any other terms).

[or]

1.      The Investor shall be entitled to participate on a pro-rata basis along with Existing Shareholders and New Investor, if any, in any proposed private sale / transfer of the equity shares of the Company by the Promoters and / or the Existing Shareholder(s) and / or New Investor, provided however that the Investor shall be entitled to a full and complete exit on a

priority basis pari passu with Existing Shareholders and New Investor in the event of any change in control as a consequence of, or in connection with, any transfer of equity shares by the Promoters such that Promoters' holding reduce below 26% of the then issued and paid-up share capital ("Tag Along Rights").

2. In the event of an exercise of a Tag-Along Right:
   i) the Investor shall not be required to provide representations and warranties
   ii) the Investor shall receive the full consideration for such shares as received by the Promoters, including non-compete consideration
   iii) the Investor shall be entitled to receive the cash equivalent of any non-cash consideration received by the Promoters and / or the Existing Shareholder(s) and / or New Investor

**Comments**

Tag-along rights, also referred to as "co-sale rights," are contractual obligations used to protect a minority shareholder, usually in a venture capital deal. If a majority shareholder sells his stake, it gives the minority shareholder the right to join the transaction and sell his minority stake in the company. Tag-alongs effectively oblige the majority shareholder to include the holdings of the minority holder in the negotiations in order to facilitate the possibility that a tag-along right is exercised.

BREAKING DOWN Tag-Along Rights

Tag-along rights are pre-negotiated rights that a minority shareholder includes in his initial issuance of a company's stock. These rights allow a minority shareholder to sell his share if a majority shareholder is negotiating a sale of his stake. Tag-along rights are prevalent in startup companies and other private firms with considerable upside potential.

Tag-along rights gives minority shareholders the ability to capitalize on a deal that a larger shareholder - often a financial institution with considerable pull - is able to put together. Large shareholders, like venture capital firms, often have a greater ability to source buyers and negotiate payment terms. Tag-along rights, therefore, provide minority shareholders with greater liquidity. This is because private equity shares are incredibly hard to sell, and majority shareholders are often able to facilitate purchases and sales on the secondary market.

Tag-along rights, also referred to as "co-sale rights," are contractual obligations used to protect a minority shareholder, usually in a venture capital deal.

Tag-along rights are pre-negotiated rights that a minority shareholder includes in his initial issuance of a company's stock. These rights allow a minority shareholder to sell his share if a majority shareholder is negotiating a sale of his stake. Tag-along rights are prevalent in startup companies and other private firms with considerable upside potential.

63. Termination

1. This Agreement may be terminated:
   a. By mutual agreement between the Parties;
   b. By either Party giving written notice in the event of material breach or default of any of the obligations by the other Party and where such breach or default has not been rectified within ninety (90) days after receipt of written notice from the other Party specifying the default;
   c. By either Party in case the other Party becomes insolvent or is declared bankrupt or goes into liquidation, voluntarily or compulsorily, except for the purpose of amalgamation or reconstruction; or
   d. If any of the Conditions Precedent have not been satisfied by [date].

2. Upon termination of this Agreement by the Licensor for a breach or default by the Licensee, all licences and rights granted under this Agreement by the Licensor to the Licensee shall be revoked and immediately cease to be effective or in force and the Licensee shall immediately cease all activities for any purpose whatsoever covered by the Licensed Patents,

the Licensed Technology, Improvement as well the Intellectual Property of the Licensor. In the event of such determination, the Licensee agrees and undertakes that it promptly return at its sole expense any and all tangible forms of information, data, material, the Licensed Patents, Improvements, the Licensed Technology on any media whatsoever to the Licensor as well as any and all copies thereof in the Licensee's possession.

3. In addition, the Licensee shall promptly remove from its premises, or from such other place utilized by the Licensee containing the property mentioned herein, any equipment, machinery, fixtures, and apparatus that incorporate any of the Licensed Technology, Improvements or inventions claimed in any of the Licensed Patents. Such removal shall be at the cost and expense of the Licensee.

4. Within twenty-four (24) hours of return or removal of the Licensor's property in accordance with this Section 24.2, the Licensee shall permit the Licensor to inspect the premises, or such other place utilized by the Licensee, including all storage media thereto.

5. Upon termination of this Agreement by efflux of time or for reasons other than solely for material breach by the Licensee, the Licensee shall have a royalty-free right to use the Licensed Patents and the Licensed Technology and to manufacture and sell the Licensed Products without any limitation period.

6. Upon the expiration or any other termination of this Agreement, the Licensee's obligations of confidentiality shall remain in full force and effect for a period of three (3) years from the date of expiration or termination.

7. Expiration or termination of this Agreement shall not relieve the Licensee from any obligations that shall or may have

accrued prior to the time such expiration or termination becomes effective.

8.  It is expressly understood and agreed by the Parties hereto that in the event of termination pursuant to the terms of this Agreement, the Party electing to terminate the Agreement shall incur no liability to the other Party hereto for damages arising solely from the exercise of the right to terminate this Agreement.

9.  The termination of this Agreement or any rights and licences granted by this Agreement, for any cause and by any party, shall be without prejudice to the remedy of the Licensor to sue for and recover any royalty or payments due up to the date of termination, and without prejudice to the remedy of either party against the other in respect of any previous or subsequent breach of any of other terms and conditions of the Agreement.

[or]

**For Shareholders Agreement:**
ARTICLE 22: TERM & TERMINATION
22.1    This Agreement shall be terminated on occurrence of one or more of the events stated in Article 22.2.
22.2    This Agreement may be terminated in accordance with the following provisions and upon the occurrence of any of the following grounds and/or events:
   (a)    By mutual written consent of the Parties; or
   (b)    Upon the bankruptcy or commencement of liquidation, assignment for the benefit of creditors or appointment into receivership of either Shareholder; or
   (c)    Upon force majeure as described in Article __ (Force Majeure), or material breach of any term(s) of this Agreement by any Party which remains unresolved and nor cured for sixty (60) days after receiving

written notice specifying condition(s) of course of conduct constituting such breach from the Party invoking its right to declare a material breach.

22.3    If this Agreement is terminated pursuant to Sub-section (b) and (c) hereinabove, the other Party have the option to purchase the bankrupt/defaulting party's interest or, if restricted by law or any regulation from buying such shares, designate a third party to acquire such shares whereupon, the provisions of Article ___.1 (Sale & Transfer of Shares) shall apply mutatis mutandis.

22.4    Termination of the Agreement by either Party shall be without prejudice to the rights that may be accrued to the either Party prior to termination and notwithstanding such termination, the Parties shall continue to be liable to each other for all acts or omissions committed prior to the termination.

### For Licensing IP agreement:

1.  This Agreement may be terminated:
    i.      By mutual agreement between the Parties;
    ii.     By either Party giving written notice in the event of material breach or default of any of the obligations by the other Party and where such breach or default has not been rectified within ninety (90) days after receipt of written notice from the other Party specifying the default;
    iii.    By either Party in case the other Party becomes insolvent or is declared bankrupt or goes into liquidation, voluntarily or compulsorily, except for the purpose of amalgamation or reconstruction; or
    iv.     If any of the Conditions Precedent have not been satisfied by [date].

2.  Upon termination of this Agreement by the Licensor for a breach or default by the Licensee, all licences and rights granted under this Agreement by the Licensor to the Licensee shall be revoked and immediately cease to be effective or in

force and the Licensee shall immediately cease all activities for any purpose whatsoever covered by the Licensed Patents, the Licensed Technology, Improvement as well the Intellectual Property of the Licensor. In the event of such determination, the Licensee agrees and undertakes that it promptly return at its sole expense any and all tangible forms of information, data, material, the Licensed Patents, Improvements, the Licensed Technology on any media whatsoever to the Licensor as well as any and all copies thereof in the Licensee's possession.

3. In addition, the Licensee shall promptly remove from its premises, or from such other place utilized by the Licensee containing the property mentioned herein, any equipment, machinery, fixtures, and apparatus that incorporate any of the Licensed Technology, Improvements or inventions claimed in any of the Licensed Patents. Such removal shall be at the cost and expense of the Licensee.

4. Within twenty-four (24) hours of return or removal of the Licensor's property in accordance with this Section 2, the Licensee shall permit the Licensor to inspect the premises, or such other place utilized by the Licensee, including all storage media thereto.

5. Upon termination of this Agreement by efflux of time or for reasons other than solely for material breach by the Licensee, the Licensee shall have a royalty-free right to use the Licensed Patents and the Licensed Technology and to manufacture and sell the Licensed Products without any limitation period.

6. Upon the expiration or any other termination of this Agreement, the Licensee's obligations of confidentiality shall remain in full force and effect for a period of three (3) years from the date of expiration or termination.

7. Expiration or termination of this Agreement shall not relieve the Licensee from any obligations that shall or may have accrued prior to the time such expiration or termination becomes effective.

8. It is expressly understood and agreed by the Parties hereto that in the event of termination pursuant to the terms of this Agreement, the Party electing to terminate the Agreement shall incur no liability to the other Party hereto for damages arising solely from the exercise of the right to terminate this Agreement.

9. The termination of this Agreement or any rights and licences granted by this Agreement, for any cause and by any party, shall be without prejudice to the remedy of the Licensor to sue for and recover any royalty or payments due up to the date of termination, and without prejudice to the remedy of either party against the other in respect of any previous or subsequent breach of any of other terms and conditions of the Agreement.

**Comments**

A contract can be terminated in various ways and under various circumstances, depending on what has been agreed upon by the parties involved and what is allowed by applicable law. Termination can have a range of effects on a contract and the parties involved, often involving the cessation of any ongoing obligations, and sometimes requiring one or both parties to fulfill certain conditions.

***Types of Termination:***
1. ***Mutual Agreement***: Both parties agree to end the contract.
2. ***Termination for Cause***: One party has breached the terms, allowing the other party to terminate the contract.
3. ***Termination Without Cause***: Some contracts allow either party to terminate without reason, often requiring notice.
4. ***Automatic Termination***: Occurs under predefined conditions set forth in the contract.

5. ***Termination by Operation of Law***: Legal reasons outside the contract can also cause termination, e.g., bankruptcy of one party, illegality, etc.

## 64. Third Party & Fiduciary Relationships
**Comments**
See "Rights of Third Parties and Fiduciary Relationships".

## 65. Warranties
Except as expressly set forth herein, any and all express and implied warranties, including but not limited to warranties of merchantability or fitness for any particular purpose or use, are expressly excluded and disclaimed.

**Comments**
A guarantee or assurance made by one party that a particular statement of fact is true. Warranties serve to allocate risk between the parties and give one party a degree of confidence in the performance or quality of the subject matter of the contract. Could be express or implied.

## 66. Waiver
The terms of this Agreement may be changed, waived, discharged, or terminated only by an instrument in writing signed by the Parties. No waiver of any term of this Agreement shall be deemed a waiver of any subsequent breach of such term or any other term of this Agreement. The failure of any Party to claim default or any part of this Agreement, or any failure to enforce any of its rights hereunder shall not be deemed a waiver of any subsequent claims or rights under this Agreement.

[or]

If at any time a Party elects not to assert its rights under any provision of this Agreement, it shall not be construed as a waiver of any of its rights hereunder.

[or]

Failure to exercise any rights under this Agreement in any one or more instances shall not constitute a waiver of such rights or any other rights in any other instances.

**Comments**
A voluntary relinquishment or surrender of some known right, claim, or privilege. In other words, one party to the contract intentionally gives up a right they have under the contract or under the law, usually by explicitly stating this in the contract itself or in a separate document. The party granting the waiver typically does so in writing, and it may be subject to certain conditions or limitations.

**== THE END ==**

... but wait for post-credits slides.

## Contract Lifecycle Management

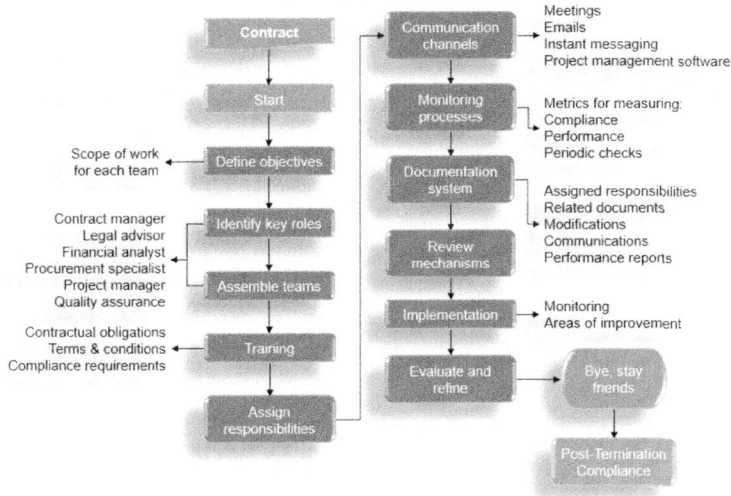

Created and designed by Yang Yen Thaw © Aug 2023

## Tips & Tricks

# Tips & Tricks

- Diplomacy is key, look for win-win negotiations
- When in doubt, be fair
- When law is silent, carries risk
- Understand the law in the contracting country
- Understand the meaning of "reasonable"
- Silence is not consent, unless there is follow up confirmation action
- Asking for forgiveness is not always easier than asking for permission
- Drafting party has advantage like white pieces in chess (cf. *contra proferentum* and *parol evidence rule*)
- Avoid cross-references in contracts, repeat if necessary
- Keep it short and simple

Created and compiled by Yang Yen Thaw © Nov 202

Business Negotiations (for Contracts as well)

# All successful contracts are from good negotiatior

## a peek preview

Following slides are extracts from the book —
Business Negotiations, by Yang Yen Thaw

Home

## What Business Negotiations are about really?

- ❏ Negotiations are about relationship building
- ❏ Chances of closing deals
- ❏ Resolving or avoiding conflicts
- ❏ For profit

Created and designed by Yang Yen Thaw © Aug 202

## Types of Negotiations (outcomes)

### Distributive Negotiation
Which results in a *zerosum game* where a party gains over the other, a win-lose game. It is a hardlined approach

### Integrative Negotiation
Which results in a *win-win game*, also called interest- or merit-based or principled negotiation. aims at adding value and reframing issues

### Mixed Motive Bargaining
There are rarely extreme distributive or integrative negotiations, this brings in mixed motive bargaining, which *includes both* distributive and integrative elements. *Win some, lose some*

© Yang Yen Thaw February 2020

| Negotiation | Bargaining |
|---|---|
| Broader term in application | Narrower term in application |
| Not all about price as quality but other factors in play | About price |
| May consist various subject matter at different points of time | One subject matter at a time |
| Cooperative in nature | Competitive in nature |
| Different interests | Same interests |
| Seeks win-win | Seeks win-lose |
| Deals with what | Deals with who |
| Deals with needs | Deals with wants |
| Different outcomes and objectives | Same product or service |
| All negotiation may be bargaining | All bargaining is not negotiation |

© Yang Yen Thaw February 2020

## Business Negotiation Styles

There can be many styles of business negotiations. Some may be a style adopted to achieve the outcome and objective and some may be strategic. Negotiating styles are listed below.

### Combative
Similar to competing, but a more aggressive, uncompromising manner.

### Factual
This style of negotiations is interrogative and objective. The negotiator using this tactic will rely totally on facts and eliminate any emotional content.

### Equitable
This style of negotiations is integrative and requires all parties to be fair and trustworthy. It looks for win -win situations.

### Relational
This style of negotiation is based more on building trust and relationships and relies on emotions. integrative and requires all parties to be fair and trustworthy. It looks for win -win situations.

### Intuitive
This style of negotiation applies convergent thinking and creative thinking. The negotiator seeks out the big picture by bringing in all ideas, specific and random, and separating key issues from irrelevant details. Intuitive negotiators can be disruptive and unpredictable because they seek innovative solutions.

© Yang Yen Thaw February 2020

# Strategies (9)

| # | Strategies | Details |
|---|-----------|---------|
| 2. | Bargaining Range | Or Bargaining Zone, is the spread between the resistance points of the negotiating parties. The concept of a bargaining range can be negative, if there is no room for settlement—or positive, if there is room for settlement |
| 3. | BATNA / WATNA | BATNA is an abbreviation of the best alternative to a negotiated agreement. Developed by negotiation researchers Roger Fisher and William Ury of the Harvard Program on Negotiation 1981, it is the perceived most advantageous alternative course of action a negotiator can take in negotiations that do not achieve the necessary outcome or objective. It is an integrative negotiation. BATNA may improve outcomes and objectives. WATNA on the other hand is the worst alternative to a negotiated agreement |
| 5. | Don't Ask, Don't Get | If terms or price is not asked for, it should be expected to be given. Therefore, ask even if not listed in agenda, and get |
| 7. | Mirroring | To repeat the counterparty's behaviour and posture to create trust and rapport |

© Yang Yen Thaw February 2020

# Tactics (26)

| # | Tactics | Details |
|---|---------|---------|
| 18. | Good Cop / Bad Cop | Parties within a negotiating party split to opposite roles with one create a hostile atmosphere or criticize or create a negative impression of the deal and the other to mitigate the circumstances or highlight the good points as positive and finally close the deal. Contrasts can sometimes help in differentiating the non-closing of the deal with the benefits of the deal *Counter:*<br>• Bring a friend.<br>• Get someone to join or ask to negotiate with only one person at a time.<br>• Call out the tactic |
| 20. | Leverage | Determining whose need is greater. Most of the engineering marvels of the world were accomplished with applied leverage. Archimedes said, "Give me a lever long enough and I shall move the world." Therefore, with a small amount of input force, we can make a great output force through leverage. *Counter:*<br>• Make factual arguments<br>• Offer small concessions as big<br>• Silence / listening is talking<br>• Offer trade-offs<br>• Ask open-ended questions |

© Yang Yen Thaw February 2020

Common Contract Clauses 2023 pub May 2001 | August 2023

All successful contracts are from good negotiations
Business Negotiations and other books by Yang Yen Thaw
available at

https://bit.ly/booksbyyt

Made in the USA
Las Vegas, NV
14 February 2025

18132028R00095